JAPANESE GRAMMAR
MADE EASY

*An Easy Step-By-Step Workbook
to Learn the Basic Japanese Grammar*

Lingo Mastery

ISBN: 978-1-951949-83-9

Copyright © 2025 by Lingo Mastery

ALL RIGHTS RESERVED

No part of this book may be reproduced, stored in a retrieval system, or transmitted in any form or by any means, electronic, mechanical, photocopying, recording, scanning, or otherwise, without the prior written permission of the publisher.

The illustrations in this book were designed using images from Freepik.com.

CONTENTS

Preface 1

Introduction 2

How to Use This Book 3

HOW TO GET THE AUDIO FILES 4

Japanese Writing System 5

あいさつ - Greetings 12

数 - Numbers 13

第一章 - LESSON 1 - Nouns in Japanese 14

    Section 1: Grammar 16

        Section 1-1: Nouns 16

        Section 1-2: Personal Pronouns 16

        Section 1-3: The Particle の 17

        Section 1-4: How to Express State-of-Being 18

        Section 1-5: Past Tense 19

        Section 1-6: Question Sentences 20

    Section 2: Vocabulary 21

    Section 3: Exercises 22

        Section 3-1: Vocabulary 22

        Section 3-2: Reading and Writing 23

        Section 3-3: Listening Exercises 29

第二章 - LESSON 2 - Describing Where Things Are 30

    Section 1: Grammar 32

        Section 1-1: Demonstrative Pronouns 32

        Section 1-2: Demonstrative Adjectives 33

        Section 1-3: あります and います 34

        Section 1-4: Question Words 36

        Section 1-5: Counters 39

Section 2: Vocabulary 42

Section 3: Exercises 43

    Section 3-1: Vocabulary 43

    Section 3-2: Reading and Writing 44

    Section 3-3: Listening Exercises 50

第三章 - LESSON 3 - Adjectives 52

Section 1: Grammar 54

    Section 1-1: Adjectives 54

    Section 1-2: Likes and Dislikes 57

    Section 1-3: How to Describe Appearance 59

    Section 1-4: *Te*-form of Adjectives 60

    Section 1-5: Adjective + なる 61

Section 2: Vocabulary 62

Section 3: Exercises 63

    Section 3-1: Vocabulary 63

    Section 3-2: Reading and Writing 64

    Section 3-3: Listening Exercises 72

第四章 - LESSON 4 - Verbs and Particles 74

Section 1: Grammar 76

    Section 1-1: Verbs in Japanese 76

    Section 1-2: Sentence Structure in Japanese 76

    Section 1-3: Present Tense 77

    Section 1-4: Frequency Adverbs 79

    Section 1-5: Past Tense 80

    Section 1-6: Particles in Japanese 81

Section 2: Vocabulary 84

Section 3: Exercises 86

    Section 3-1: Vocabulary 86

    Section 3-2: Reading and Writing 87

    Section 3-3: Listening Exercises 96

第五章 - LESSON 5 - *Te*-form of Verbs in Japanese ... 98

Section 1: Grammar ... 100

Section 1-1: How to Make *Te*-form ... 100
Section 1-2: Various Ways of Using the *Te*-form ... 101
Section 1-3: Using *Te*-form to Describe More Than Two Activities ... 104
Section 1-4: How to Explain What You Have Done Already ... 105

Section 2: Vocabulary ... 106

Section 3: Exercises ... 107

Section 3-1: Vocabulary ... 107
Section 3-2: Reading and Writing ... 108
Section 3-3: Listening Exercises ... 116

第六章 - LESSON 6 - Short Form ... 118

Section 1: Grammar ... 120

Section 1-1: Present Tense Short Form ... 120
Section 1-2: Informal Speech ... 121
Section 1-3: Past Tense Short Form ... 122
Section 1-4: Various Usages of Short Form ... 123
Section 1-5: How to Explain Reasons ... 125

Section 2: Vocabulary ... 127

Section 3: Exercises ... 128

Section 3-1: Vocabulary ... 129
Section 3-2: Reading and Writing ... 129
Section 3-3: Listening Exercises ... 141

第七章 - LESSON 7 - Describe What You Want to Do ... 142

Section 1: Grammar ... 144

Section 1-1: Describe What You Want to Do ... 144
Section 1-2: Describe What Someone Else Wants to Do ... 146
Section 1-3: Things You Want ... 147
Section 1-4: Using "When..." ... 149
Section 1-5: Describing the Purpose of Movement ... 149

Section 2: Vocabulary **151**

Section 3: Exercises **152**

    Section 3-1: Vocabulary 152
    Section 3-2: Reading and Writing 153
    Section 3-3: Listening Exercises 164

Conclusion **165**

Answer Key **167**

PREFACE

Japanese Grammar Made Easy is a workbook for beginners in the study of the Japanese language. The book covers basic grammar that appears frequently in the Japanese Language Proficiency Test (JLPT) N5.

After carefully examining the existing language learning books on the market and having discussions with experienced Japanese language teachers, we have concluded that a new student-friendly and easy-to-understand grammar workbook is sorely needed. The aim of this book is to help students build a solid grammatical foundation without using convoluted grammatical terminology. Students are encouraged to think in Japanese by focusing on sentence patterns and practicing grammar in context. We have designed the book in such a way that previous grammatical knowledge is not necessary and students can learn the language intuitively with an abundance of examples.

Since this book contains an extensive number of example sentences in Japanese, we strongly recommend students to start and finish the workbook *"Lingo Mastery: Japanese Hiragana and Katakana Made Easy."* This will greatly assist students in building reading and writing skills in hiragana and katakana before studying Japanese grammar.

Furigana has been added above all kanji characters that appear in this book so that students can read and understand the example sentences without knowing any kanji characters.

The book has been designed with the purpose of being a self-study workbook; however, it is also ideal for use in a classroom setting.

It is our sincere hope and desire that this book becomes a powerful tool in the hands of thousands of students and that it enables them to better understand Japanese sentence structures and, last but in no way least, to have fun expressing their thoughts in Japanese.

INTRODUCTION

It is often said that Japanese is one of the most difficult languages in the world. This simple statement can intimidate many language learners and give them an excuse to give up. But is it really hard to learn Japanese?

It is safe to say that Japanese is very different from any European language, such as English, German or Spanish. For example, Japanese has three writing systems – hiragana, katakana and kanji – which are Chinese characters. It may take time to memorize forty-six basic hiragana and katakana characters. Also, there are more than 2,000 kanji characters that you need to learn to be a fluent reader of Japanese content.

Understandably, that may sound very daunting for some learners. It is true that the sentence structure is also quite different from that of English. For example, English uses the so-called SVO (subject–verb–object) sentence structure. On the other hand, Japanese uses the SOV sentence structure which means that the verb always comes at the end.

All these facts, however, should not lead us to assume that the Japanese language is harder than any other language. There are a number of things that make Japanese easier. For example, in Japanese there is no use of gender and no plural or singular. Conjugation of verbs is fairly simple. Unlike a number of languages in the world, the verb stays the same regardless of who does that action. There is one single verb form for each tense.

Therefore, keep in mind that Japanese is not necessarily more difficult, but just different from English. By learning basic Japanese grammar and vocabulary with this book, forming sentences and becoming a fluent Japanese speaker will become a reachable goal for students.

For this reason, in this book, we have consciously endeavored to use easy-to-understand grammar explanations, and numerous example sentences have been used extensively. The work has been done for you, your task at hand is to read and form new thinking patterns using new sentence structures.

HOW TO USE THIS BOOK

This book, *"Japanese Grammar Made Easy"*, consists of seven chapters and each chapter has three sections. Below is a brief description of each of the three sections:

Section 1: Grammar

The book begins with grammar explanations. Numerous example sentences are provided. Basic kanji characters with furigana are used in the example sentences so that students can get used to kanji in Japanese writing. Read them carefully.

Section 2 : Vocabulary

The vocabulary section presents all the new words you will find in that chapter. The vocabulary box helps learners to set a goal to memorize vocabulary for each chapter.

Section 3 : Exercises

This section provides two types of activities: writing and reading, as well as listening. In the writing and reading exercises, you will practice how to conjugate verbs and adjectives, forming simple sentences and reading the contents. When it comes to listening exercises, audio recordings are provided and students can develop their listening skills and practice taking notes in Japanese.

Students are encouraged to start studying this book from chapter one since the book is designed in logical order. By finishing each chapter, one by one, students can build grammatical structures of the Japanese language systematically.

 This headphone symbol next to a paragraph or dialogue indicates that audio content is available for the corresponding section.

 This headphone with a pencil next to an exercise means that you will need to refer to the corresponding audio content to complete the exercise.

HOW TO GET THE AUDIO FILES

Some of the exercises throughout this book come with accompanying audio files. You can download these audio files if you head over to:
www.lingomastery.com/japanese-gme-audio

If you're having trouble downloading the audio, contact us at
www.lingomastery.com/contact

JAPANESE WRITING SYSTEM

The Japanese language has three types of writing systems: hiragana, katakana, and kanji. Lists of basic hiragana and katakana characters are provided below. A more detailed explanation about the Japanese writing system can be found in Lingo Mastery's *"Japanese Hiragana and Katakana Made Easy."*

Hiragana

Hiragana is a phonetic alphabetic system that is mainly used for native Japanese words, conjugating verbs, and grammatical particles. A total of 46 hiragana characters are used in the Japanese writing system.

あ	い	う	え	お
a	i	u	e	o
か	き	く	け	こ
ka	ki	ku	ke	ko
さ	し	す	せ	そ
sa	shi	su	se	so
た	ち	つ	て	と
ta	chi	tsu	te	to
な	に	ぬ	ね	の
na	ni	nu	ne	no
は	ひ	ふ	へ	ほ
ha (wa)	hi	fu	he (e)	ho
ま	み	む	め	も
ma	mi	mu	me	mo
や		ゆ		よ
ya		yu		yo
ら	り	る	れ	ろ
ra	ri	ru	re	ro
わ				を
wa				wo
ん				
n				

Hiragana with diacritical marks and contracted sounds

Additionally, hiragana makes use of two diacritical marks. The two small dashes (゛) are called *dakuten* (濁点). The small circle (゜) is called *handakuten* (半濁点). By adding these diacritical marks onto the hiragana characters, you can change the sound of the character. With the *dakuten* (゛), the consonants *k, s, t, h* become the consonants *g, z, d, b*, respectively. The consonant h changes to a p sound with *handakuten* (゜). Look at the chart below.

が	ぎ	ぐ	げ	ご
ga	gi	gu	ge	go
ざ	じ	ず	ぜ	ぞ
za	ji	zu	ze	zo
だ	ぢ	づ	で	ど
da	ji	zu	de	do
ば	び	ぶ	べ	ぼ
ba	bi	bu	be	bo
ぱ	ぴ	ぷ	ぺ	ぽ
pa	pi	pu	pe	po

When the hiragana characters や, ゆ and よ are written in smaller size, they take on a new function, transcribing contracted sounds. In the chart below, you will see all hiragana characters with the small や, ゆ and よ.

きゃ	きゅ	きょ
kya	kyu	kyo
しゃ	しゅ	しょ
sha	shu	sho
ちゃ	ちゅ	ちょ
cha	chu	cho
にゃ	にゅ	にょ
nya	nyu	nyo
ひゃ	ひゅ	ひょ
hya	hyu	hyo
みゃ	みゅ	みょ
mya	myu	myo
りゃ	りゅ	りょ
rya	ryu	ryo
びゃ	びゅ	びょ
bya	byu	byo
ぴゃ	ぴゅ	ぴょ
pya	pyu	pyo
ぎゃ	ぎゅ	ぎょ
gya	gyu	gyo
じゃ	じゅ	じょ
ja	ju	jo

Katakana

Katakana is also a phonetic alphabetic system. It has 46 corresponding characters that make the same sounds as found in hiragana. The major difference is that katakana is used for loanwords and foreign names.

ア	イ	ウ	エ	オ
a	i	u	e	o
カ	キ	ク	ケ	コ
ka	ki	ku	ke	ko
サ	シ	ス	セ	ソ
sa	shi	su	se	so
タ	チ	ツ	テ	ト
ta	chi	tsu	te	to
ナ	ニ	ヌ	ネ	ノ
na	ni	nu	ne	no
ハ	ヒ	フ	ヘ	ホ
ha (wa)	hi	fu	he (e)	ho
マ	ミ	ム	メ	モ
ma	mi	mu	me	mo
ヤ		ユ		ヨ
ya		yu		yo
ラ	リ	ル	レ	ロ
ra	ri	ru	re	ro
ワ				ヲ
wa				wo
ン				
n				

Katakana with diacritical marks and contracted sounds

In the chart below, you will see all 25 katakana characters with diacritical marks and the corresponding letters of the alphabet.

ガ	ギ	グ	ゲ	ゴ
ga	gi	gu	ge	go
ザ	ジ	ズ	ゼ	ゾ
za	ji	zu	ze	zo
ダ	ヂ	ヅ	デ	ド
da	ji	zu	de	do
バ	ビ	ブ	ベ	ボ
ba	bi	bu	be	bo
パ	ピ	プ	ペ	ポ
pa	pi	pu	pe	po

You will see all katakana contracted sounds in the chart below. The pronunciations are the same as in hiragana.

キャ	キュ	キョ
kya	kyu	kyo
シャ	シュ	ショ
sha	shu	sho
チャ	チュ	チョ
cha	chu	cho
ニャ	ニュ	ニョ
nya	nyu	nyo
ヒャ	ヒュ	ヒョ
hya	hyu	hyo
ミャ	ミュ	ミョ
mya	myu	myo
リャ	リュ	リョ
rya	ryu	ryo
ギャ	ギュ	ギョ
gya	gyu	gyo
ジャ	ジュ	ジョ
ja	ju	jo
ビャ	ビュ	ビョ
bya	byu	byo
ピャ	ピュ	ピョ
pya	pyu	pyo

Basics of Kanji Characters

The word kanji in Japanese literally means "Han character" or "Chinese character." They were introduced to Japan back when the Japanese language did not yet have its own writing system. As of 2023, the Japanese government listed a total of 2,136 kanji characters as *Jōyō kanji* (Commonly Used Kanji). Students in Japan are expected to learn all of them during their compulsory education, which includes elementary and junior high school.

There are four categories of kanji and they reference the way characters originally came to be.

1. Pictograph: Kanji characters that originated from pictures of objects.

Example: 木 (tree), 山 (mountain), 川 (river)

2. Indicator: These kanji characters translate abstract concepts into symbols.

Example: 一 (one), 上 (top), 下 (bottom)

3. Compound ideographs: This category of kanji is formed by combining two or more existing kanji characters.

Example: 日 (sun) + 月 (moon) = 明 (bright)

4. Phonetic ideographic characters: Kanji made up of one-part sound and one-part meaning.

Example: 艹 (grass: meaning) + 化 (ka: sound) = 花 (flower)

Most kanji characters have multiple readings, which are divided into two types. The first type is the original Chinese pronunciation, which we call the on-reading (on-yomi) and the second is the kun-reading (kun-yomi) that is the native Japanese pronunciation for the same character.

See the examples below.

人 person	On-reading	Kun-reading
	ジン、ニン	ひと

友 friend	On-reading	Kun-reading
	ユウ	とも

Since one kanji character has multiple readings, sometimes hiragana characters are added right above the kanji character to show how kanji characters are intended to be read in the context. These hiragana characters are called furigana. In this book, furigana is added above all kanji characters to assist learners who have not yet started learning them.

あいさつ
GREETINGS

 Greetings are important in all cultures and usually they are the first thing to study when learning a new language. To get you started, we have provided the 20 most common Japanese greetings. Listen to the audio recordings and repeat.   (Find audio on page 4.)

おはよう。	Good morning.
おはようございます。	Good morning. (polite)
こんにちは。	Good afternoon.
こんばんは。	Good evening.
またね。	See you later.
失礼^{しつれい}します。	Goodbye.
おやすみ。	Good night.
おやすみなさい。	Good night. (polite)
ありがとう。	Thank you.
ありがとうございます。	Thank you very much. (polite)
すみません。	Excuse me. / I'm sorry.
いってきます。	I'm leaving. See you later.
いってらっしゃい。	Please go and come back.
ただいま。	I'm home.
おかえりなさい。	Welcome home.
いただきます。	Thank you (for the meal just served); I received (this meal)
ごちそうさまでした。	Thank you for the meal. (after eating)
はじめまして。	Nice to meet you.
よろしくおねがいします。	Thank you in advance.
もしもし…	Hello. (on the phone)
ようこそ。	Welcome!
いらっしゃいませ。	Welcome. (store, restaurant, office)

数 (かず)
NUMBERS (Find audio on page 4.)

0	ぜろ / れい				
1	いち	11	じゅういち	30	さんじゅう
2	に	12	じゅうに	40	よんじゅう
3	さん	13	じゅうさん	50	ごじゅう
4	し / よん	14	じゅうし / じゅうよん	60	ろくじゅう
5	ご	15	じゅうご	70	ななじゅう
6	ろく	16	じゅうろく	80	はちじゅう
7	なな / しち	17	じゅうなな / じゅうしち	90	きゅうじゅう
8	はち	18	じゅうはち	100	ひゃく
9	きゅう / く	19	じゅうきゅう / じゅうく		
10	じゅう	20	にじゅう		

100	ひゃく	1000	せん	10000	いちまん
200	にひゃく	2000	にせん	20000	にまん
300	さんびゃく	3000	さんぜん	30000	さんまん
400	よんひゃく	4000	よんせん	40000	よんまん
500	ごひゃく	5000	ごせん	50000	ごまん
600	ろっぴゃく	6000	ろくせん	60000	ろくまん
700	ななひゃく	7000	ななせん	70000	ななまん
800	はっぴゃく	8000	はっせん	80000	はちまん
900	きゅうひゃく	9000	きゅうせん	90000	きゅうまん

第一章
だいいっしょう
LESSON 1

NOUNS IN JAPANESE

もくひょう 目標	**OBJECTIVE**

✓ Learn how to express state-of-being.
✓ Learn how to make question sentences.

ないよう 内容	**CONTENTS**

Section 1: Grammar

Section 1-1: Nouns

Section 1-2: Personal pronouns

Section 1-3: The particle の

Section 1-4: How to express state-of-being

Section 1-5: Past tense

Section 1-6: Question sentences: 〜か?

Section 2: Vocabulary

Section 3: Exercises

SECTION 1: GRAMMAR

SECTION 1-1: NOUNS

A noun describes things, people, places, times, abstract concepts, and so forth.

Things
スマホ　smartphone

Places
図書館 (としょかん)　library

People
学生 (がくせい)　student

Time
日曜日 (にちようび)　Sunday

Unlike in English, nouns in Japanese are not accompanied by any articles such as "a," "an," and "the." Another difference is that there are no words in Japanese that correspond to the plural "-s" at the end of a noun.

SECTION 1-2: PERSONAL PRONOUNS

Personal pronouns are words used to address or refer to present people or things, such as "I," "he," and "she." There are various ways to refer to yourself. The most common personal pronouns to refer to yourself are 私 **(watashi)**, 僕 **(boku)**, and 俺 **(ore).** Let's see the difference among each of these pronouns.

While **watashi** is a genderless and formal personal pronoun that can be used in a business setting, **boku**, on the other hand, sounds casual and is mostly used by men. **Ore** is even more casual and masculine than the pronoun **boku**, which can be used in casual settings.

In Japanese, the second person pronoun "you" is **anata**. The third person pronoun "he" is **kare** and the pronoun "she" is **kanojo**. However, Japanese native speakers do not use these personal pronouns too often. Rather than using these personal pronouns, native speakers prefer using their own names in conversation. The reason is that in Japanese, constantly calling the listener **anata** in every sentence may sound rude as if you are accusing the person of something. **Kare** and **kanojo** also can mean "boyfriend" and "girlfriend." Therefore, Japanese speakers generally use their own names to avoid any confusion.

In the case of pluralizing personal pronouns, simply add たち **(tachi)** after each personal pronoun. The only exception is **karera**, which means "they" referring to males (could be a group of males and females, too) in English. Instead of たち, ら is added after **kare**. However, **karera** is not commonly used.

Singular		Plural	
わたし 私	I (both men and women)	わたし 私たち	we
ぼく 僕	I (mostly for men)	ぼく 僕たち	we
おれ 俺	I (casual, mostly for men)	おれ 俺たち	we
あなた	you	あなたたち	you
かれ 彼	he	かれ 彼ら	they (male, or male and female)
かのじょ 彼女	she	かのじょ 彼女たち	they (female)

SECTION 1-3: PARTICLE の

The function of the particle の is to connect two nouns. One of the main ways to use this particle is to indicate possession. It acts like the possessive "'s" or "of" in English. As explained in the previous grammar point, わたし **watashi** is "I" in English. If you add the particle の at the end of the pronoun, its meaning becomes "my." See the examples below.

わたし 私	I	わたし 私の〜	my…
あなた	you	あなたの〜	your…
はは 母	mother	はは 母の〜	my mother's…
ジョン	John	ジョンの〜	John's…

Examples:

わたし
私 の スマホ   my smartphone

わたし はは ほん
私 の 母 の 本   my mother's book

ふく
ジョン の 服   John's clothing

However, this particle has more functions. Examples are provided below to show how this particle connects two nouns.

<ruby>日本<rt>にほん</rt></ruby><u>の</u><ruby>学校<rt>がっこう</rt></ruby>　a school in Japan

<ruby>大学<rt>だいがく</rt></ruby><u>の</u><ruby>先生<rt>せんせい</rt></ruby>　a college professor

<ruby>東京<rt>とうきょう</rt></ruby><u>の</u>おみやげ　a souvenir from Tokyo

In the examples above, the particle の cannot be translated into the possessive "'s" or "of" in English. But keep in mind that the main idea comes at the end and the first noun gives more information about the second noun. In the first example above, the second noun *Gakkou* (学校) is the main idea and the first noun *Nihon* (日本) makes it more specific. In this case, it gives us the specific location.

details of noun 2		main idea
Noun1	の	Noun2

SECTION 1-4: HOW TO EXPRESS STATE-OF-BEING

Now, let's learn how to express state-of-being in Japanese. "I am Sandy," "John is a student," "I am American." These sentences, which don't contain verbs, can be formed by using the following grammar pattern. Keep in mind that there is no verb for the state-of-being, like the verbs "am" or "is" in English. Rather, you can declare what it is by attaching です at the end of sentences.

$$X \text{ is } Y \quad \rightarrow \quad X \text{ は } Y \text{ です}$$

Examples

<ruby>私<rt>わたし</rt></ruby>はサンディです。　I am Sandy.

ジョンは<ruby>学生<rt>がくせい</rt></ruby>です。　John is a student.

<ruby>私<rt>わたし</rt></ruby>はアメリカ<ruby>人<rt>じん</rt></ruby>です。　I am an American.

In Japanese, personal pronouns can be omitted when it's clear who the speaker is talking about. See the examples below.

サンディです。　(I am) Sandy.

私の車です。　(It is) my car.

日本人です。　(I am) Japanese.

How about the negative form? Use the following grammar pattern to express something that is not X.

X is not Y　→　X は Y じゃないです / じゃありません / ではありません

There are mainly three variations of the negative form: the first form, じゃないです, is casual and colloquial. The second, じゃありません, is formal. The last, ではありません, is appropriate for writing.

Examples

ジョンは学生じゃないです。　John is not a student.

私はアメリカ人ではありません。　I am not an American.

SECTION 1-5: PAST TENSE

To make sentences using the past tense, です is replaced with でした *deshita*. The negative form じゃないです is replaced with じゃなかったです. See the following box and the example sentences.

X was Y　→　X は Y でした

X wasn't Y　→　X は Y じゃなかったです

Examples

ジョンは学生(がくせい)でした。　John was a student.

母(はは)は主婦(しゅふ)じゃなかったです。　My mother was not a housewife.

Instead of じゃなかったです, じゃありませんでした can also be used. ではなかったです and ではありませんでした are appropriate for writing.

SECTION 1-6: QUESTION SENTENCES

To form questions in Japanese, a hiragana character か is added at the end of each sentence. See the examples below. Take note that it is not customary to write the question mark at the end of a question sentence in Japanese.

日本人(にほんじん)です。　(I am) Japanese.

日本人(にほんじん)ですか？　(Are you) Japanese?

ジョンさんは大学生(だいがくせい)です。　John is a college student.

ジョンさんは大学生(だいがくせい)ですか？　Is John a college student?

（これは）サンディのカメラです。　(It is) Sandy's camera.

（これは）サンディのカメラですか？　(Is it) Sandy's camera?

SECTION 2: VOCABULARY

This section reviews all the vocabulary used in the example sentences from section 1 and additional vocabulary. We encourage you to try to memorize all vocabulary in this section.

Objects

スマートフォン（スマホ）　smartphone

<ruby>本<rt>ほん</rt></ruby>　book

<ruby>服<rt>ふく</rt></ruby>　clothing

カメラ　camera

お<ruby>土産<rt>みやげ</rt></ruby>　souvenir

<ruby>写真<rt>しゃしん</rt></ruby>　picture, photo

<ruby>車<rt>くるま</rt></ruby>　car

<ruby>家<rt>いえ</rt></ruby>　house

<ruby>犬<rt>いぬ</rt></ruby>　dog

People

お<ruby>母<rt>かあ</rt></ruby>さん / <ruby>母<rt>はは</rt></ruby>　mother

お<ruby>父<rt>とう</rt></ruby>さん / <ruby>父<rt>ちち</rt></ruby>　father

お<ruby>兄<rt>にい</rt></ruby>ちゃん / <ruby>兄<rt>あに</rt></ruby>　older brother

お<ruby>姉<rt>ねえ</rt></ruby>ちゃん / <ruby>姉<rt>あね</rt></ruby>　older sister

<ruby>弟<rt>おとうと</rt></ruby>　younger brother

<ruby>妹<rt>いもうと</rt></ruby>　younger sister

<ruby>家族<rt>かぞく</rt></ruby>　family

School

<ruby>学生<rt>がくせい</rt></ruby>　student

<ruby>先生<rt>せんせい</rt></ruby>　teacher

<ruby>学校<rt>がっこう</rt></ruby>　school

<ruby>大学<rt>だいがく</rt></ruby>　college, university

<ruby>大学生<rt>だいがくせい</rt></ruby>　college/university student

Locations

<ruby>図書館<rt>としょかん</rt></ruby>　library

<ruby>東京<rt>とうきょう</rt></ruby>　Tokyo

Countries

<ruby>日本<rt>にほん</rt></ruby>　Japan

<ruby>中国<rt>ちゅうごく</rt></ruby>　China

<ruby>韓国<rt>かんこく</rt></ruby>　Korea

アメリカ　America

カナダ　Canada

オーストラリア　Australia

イギリス　United Kingdom

<ruby>南<rt>みなみ</rt></ruby>アフリカ　South Africa

メキシコ　Mexico

〜<ruby>人<rt>じん</rt></ruby>　…people (e.g., フランス<ruby>人<rt>じん</rt></ruby>　French people/person)

Occupations

<ruby>仕事<rt>しごと</rt></ruby> / <ruby>職業<rt>しょくぎょう</rt></ruby>　job, work

<ruby>会社員<rt>かいしゃいん</rt></ruby>　office worker

<ruby>医者<rt>いしゃ</rt></ruby>　doctor

エンジニア　engineer

<ruby>主婦<rt>しゅふ</rt></ruby>　housewife

<ruby>大工<rt>だいく</rt></ruby>　carpenter

SECTION 3: EXERCISES

SECTION 3-1: VOCABULARY

Practice 1: 単語(たんご)を覚(おぼ)えよう

Match the vocabulary that corresponds to the pictures.

① おみやげ •

② 服(ふく) •

③ カメラ •

④ 先生(せんせい) •

⑤ 学校(がっこう) •

⑥ 医者(いしゃ) •

⑦ 大工(だいく) •

⑧ イギリス •

SECTION 3-2: READING AND WRITING

Practice 1: The particle の

Translate the following phrases into Japanese using the particle の.

① my dog _____

② my camera _____

③ my car _____

④ my father _____

⑤ my younger brother _____

⑥ Sandy's house _____

⑦ a student in Canada _____

⑧ a college in Japan _____

⑨ a picture of a car _____

⑩ a school library _____

Practice 2: 文を作ろう

Rearrange the following sentences in the correct order.

① です / は / 私 / 学生

_____

② 弟 / は / です / 大学生

_____

③ です / 兄 / は / ２０才

_____

④ 父 / です / は / 会社員

_____

⑤ は / 母 / です / 主婦

_____

Practice 3: 文(ぶん)を書(か)こう

Translate the sentence below using the vocabulary provided below.

① 車(くるま)

That is my car.
_____

That is not my car.
_____

② お母(かあ)さん

She is my mother.
_____

She is not my mother.
_____

③ お兄(にい)さん

He is my older brother.
_____

He is not my older brother.
_____

④ イギリス人(じん)

I am British.
_____

I am not British.
_____

⑤ 学校(がっこう)

That is my school.
_____

That is not my school.
_____

⑥ 大学生(だいがくせい)

I am a college student.
_____

I am not a college student.
_____

⑦ エンジニア

My father is an engineer.
_____

My father is not an engineer.
_____

⑧ １８才(さい)

My younger brother is 18 years old.
_____

My younger brother is not 18 years old.
_____

Practice 4: 質問(しつもん)しよう

Below are answer statements. Provide the appropriate questions for each of them.

① Q:_____
　A: ジョンです。

② Q:_____
　A: はい、私(わたし)は大学生(だいがくせい)です。

③ Q:_____
　A: はい、わたしのスマホです。

④ Q:_____
　A: はい、日本人(にほんじん)です。

⑤ Q:_____
　A: はい、アメリカの写真(しゃしん)です。

⑥ Q:_____
　A: はい、学校(がっこう)の先生(せんせい)でした。

⑦ Q:_____
　A: いいえ、サンディの車(くるま)じゃありません。

Practice 5: 質問(しつもん)に答(こた)えよう

Meet the students from the Japanese language school. Examine the chart below and answer the questions that follow.

Name	Sandy サンディ	Diana ディアナ	John ジョン	Alex アレックス	Toshi トシ
Nationality	South African	Mexican	American	Australian	Japanese
Occupation	office worker	doctor	engineer	student	teacher

Example:

Question: サンディは会社員(かいしゃいん)ですか？

Answer: はい、サンディはかいしゃいんです。

① サンディはアメリカ人ですか？

_____

② ディアナはメキシコ人ですか？

_____

③ ジョンは会社員(かいしゃいん)ですか？

_____

④ アレックスは学生(がくせい)ですか？

_____

⑤ トシは先生(せんせい)ですか？

_____

26 Section 3 | Lesson 1 | *Japanese Grammar Made Easy*

Practice 6: みんなの自己紹介

Read the self-introductions of each student. Match the information box with the letters A-E corresponding to each student.

A

はじめまして。

私は日本人です。

日本語の先生です。

よろしくおねがいします。

B

はじめまして。

私は南アフリカ人です。

私は会社員です。

よろしくおねがいします。

C

はじめまして。

私はアメリカ人です。

仕事はエンジニアです。

よろしくおねがいします。

D

はじめまして。

私はメキシコ人です。

職業は医者です。

よろしくおねがいします。

E

はじめまして。

私はオーストラリア人です。

学生です。

よろしくおねがいします。

サンディ
(　　)

ディアナ
(　　)

ジョン
(　　)

アレックス
(　　)

トシ
(　　)

Practice 7: 自己紹介しよう
_{じこしょうかい}

Write your own introduction.

はじめまして！

_____(name)

_____(nationality)

_____(student or occupation)

_____(age)

Practice 8: 過去形の文
_{かこけい ぶん}

Change the following sentences into the past tense.

① 私は学生です。
_{わたし がくせい}

_____

② お父さんは学校の先生です。
_{とう がっこう せんせい}

_____

③ お母さんは主婦じゃないです。
_{かあ しゅふ}

_____

④ 兄は会社員じゃありません。
_{あに かいしゃいん}

_____

⑤ お姉ちゃんは大学生です。
_{ねえ だいがくせい}

_____

28   Section 3 | Lesson 1 | *Japanese Grammar Made Easy*

SECTION 3-3: LISTENING EXERCISES

 Practice 1: 自己紹介を聴き取ろう (Find audio on page 4.)

The students of the Japanese language school are introducing themselves. Listen to the audio recording and fill in the answers in the chart below.

① ② ③ ④

Name	Nationality	Occupation/School	Age
① フアン Juan			
② ノア Noa			
③ スカイ Sky			
④ ソア Soa			

 Practice 2: 私の家族 (Find audio on page 4.)

One of the students, Soa, shows a picture of her family to other students. Listen to the audio recordings and indicate if the sentences are true or false.

① お父さんは韓国人です。

(True/False)

② お母さんは主婦です。

(True/False)

③ 弟は大学生です。

(True/False)

第二章
LESSON 2
だいにしょう

DESCRIBING WHERE THINGS ARE

| もくひょう
目標 | **OBJECTIVE** |

✓ Learn the difference between demonstrative adjectives.
✓ Learn how to describe where things are.
✓ Learn how to ask questions.
✓ Learn essential Japanese counters.

| ないよう
内容 | **CONTENTS** |

Section 1: Grammar

Section 1-1: Demonstrative Pronouns

Section 1-2: Demonstrative Adjectives

Section 1-3: あります and います

Section 1-4: Question Words

Section 1-5: Counters

Section 2: Vocabulary

Section 3: Exercises

SECTION 1: GRAMMAR

SECTION 1-1: DEMONSTRATIVE PRONOUNS

A demonstrative pronoun is used to point to a specific person or thing; some examples in English are: this, that, these, and those. In Japanese, the three most commonly used demonstrative pronouns are **kore**, **sore**, and **are**. See the differences among these demonstrative pronouns in Japanese.

English	Japanese	How to use
this	これ	**Kore** refers to something that is close to the speaker.
that	それ	**Sore** indicates something that is close to the listener.
that	あれ	**Are** shows something that is far from both the speaker and listener.

Examples:

これは私(わたし)のかばんです。　This is my bag.

それはアレックス君(くん)のかさです。　That is Alex's umbrella.

あれはジョンさんの家(いえ)です。　That is John's house.

In the box below are additional commonly used pronouns. The pronouns **koko, soko,** and **asoko** are used to refer to places. The pronouns **kocchi, socchi,** and **acchi** are words to explain direction in the informal settings. In the formal settings, **kochira, sochira,** and **achira** should be used.

English	Japanese	English	Japanese (casual)	Japanese (formal)
here	ここ	this way, here	こっち	こちら
there	そこ	that way, there	そっち	そちら
over there	あそこ	that way, over there	あっち	あちら

ここは図書館（としょかん）です。　Here is the library.

ジョンさんの家（いえ）はあそこです。　John's house is over there.

こっちに来（き）て！　Come here!

SECTION 1-2: DEMONSTRATIVE ADJECTIVES

A demonstrative adjective is always followed by a noun. In English, the demonstrative pronouns this, that, these, and those can be used as demonstrative adjectives as well. However, in Japanese when a demonstrative pronoun is followed by a noun, different words are used. There are three Japanese demonstrative adjectives: **kono, sono,** and **ano**. The following box shows how to use these three demonstrative adjectives.

English	Japanese	How to use
This + noun	この + noun	Refers to something or a person that is close to the speaker.
That + noun	その + noun	Indicates something or a person that is close to the listener.
That + noun	あの + noun	Shows something or person that is far from both the speaker and listener.

Examples:

<ruby>この<rt></rt></ruby><ruby>時計<rt>とけい</rt></ruby>は<ruby>私<rt>わたし</rt></ruby>のです。　This clock is mine.

そのくつは５０００<ruby>円<rt>えん</rt></ruby>です。　Those shoes are 5,000 yen.

あのかばんはいくらですか？　How much does that bag cost?

SECTION 1-3: あります AND います

The verbs **arimasu** and **imasu** are used to express the existence of something. The verb あります is used for plants and non-living things, such as buildings, computers, or cameras. On the other hand, the verb います is used for living things, such as family members, teachers, and animals. This is similar to the English expression, there is/are.

Examples:

スタバがあります。　There is a Starbucks.

<ruby>犬<rt>いぬ</rt></ruby>がいます。　There is a dog.

	There is/are…	
	affirmative	negative
non-living things	〜があります	〜がありません
living things	〜がいます	〜がいません

Note that the verbs **arimasu** and **imasu** usually come with a particle が.

Arimasu and **imasu** also can be used to express possession of something: **arimasu** for non-living things and **imasu** for living things.

Examples:

エアコンがあります。	There is an air conditioner. (non-living thing)
<ruby>時間<rt>じかん</rt></ruby>がありません。	I don't have time. (non-living thing)
<ruby>日本人<rt>にほんじん</rt></ruby>の<ruby>友<rt>とも</rt></ruby>だちがいます。	I have a Japanese friend. (living thing)

時間 (じかん)
日本人 (にほんじん) 友 (とも)

When describing where something is specifically, add the location with the particle に prior to the thing you are mentioning.

学校（がっこう）にエアコンがあります。　There are air conditioners <u>at school</u>.

あそこにスタバがあります。　There is a Starbucks coffee shop <u>over there</u>.

（location）に（something/person）があります／います

Below is a list of useful vocabulary to describe locations.

English	Japanese	English	Japanese
on, above	上 (うえ)	near	近く (ちか)
under, beneath	下 (した)	next to	隣 (となり)
to the right of	右 (みぎ)	north	北 (きた)
to the left of	左 (ひだり)	south	南 (みなみ)
in front of	前 (まえ)	west	西 (にし)
behind	後ろ (うし)	east	東 (ひがし)
inside	中 (なか)		

つくえの上に本があります。　There is a book <u>on the desk</u>.

引き出しの中にはさみがあります。　There are scissors <u>inside the drawer</u>.

図書館の隣にレストランがあります。　There is a restaurant <u>next to the library</u>.

SECTION 1-4: QUESTION WORDS

As covered in the lesson 1, to form a question sentence, you simply need to add the question marker か *(ka)* at the end of each sentence. Sometimes question sentences may contain question words, such as *what, where, when, why, who,* or *which.* See the list of Japanese question words.

Question words	Japanese
What	何　（なに、なん）
Where	どこ
When	いつ
Why	なぜ、どうして、なんで
Who	だれ
Which	どっち、どれ、どちら
How	どう、どのように
How many	いくつ
How much (price)	いくら
How much (amount)	どのくらい

In English, question words generally appear at the beginning of sentences; for example, "What is this?" or "When are you going to eat?" However, Japanese question words replace the corresponding noun, without changing position in the sentence. See the example below.

これは<u>私のかさ</u>です。　　This is my umbrella.

これは<u>何</u>ですか？　　What is this?

Watashi no kasa (my umbrella) is replaced with **nan** (what) and the question marker か is added.

Below are some example sentences for each of the question words.

1. What 何（なに、なん）

The question word "what" in Japanese has two pronunciations, **nani** and **nan**. **Nani** is usually used before a particle and **nan** is used right before the auxiliary verb **desu** or before a counter such as **ji** (o'clock) or **sai** (age). Therefore, the words **nan-sai** mean "how old" and **nan-ji** means "what time is it."

しゅみは<ruby>何<rt>なん</rt></ruby>ですか？　What are your hobbies?

<ruby>今<rt>いま</rt></ruby>、<ruby>何時<rt>なんじ</rt></ruby>ですか？　What time is it now?

<ruby>何才<rt>なんさい</rt></ruby>ですか？　How old (are you)?

2. Where どこ

The question word どこ **(doko)** is used to ask for a location when you are traveling.

トイレはどこですか？　Where is the bathroom?

<ruby>図書館<rt>としょかん</rt></ruby>はどこですか？　Where is the library?

3. When いつ

The question word いつ **(itsu)** is used to ask "when" to show when an event will take place.

<ruby>誕生日<rt>たんじょうび</rt></ruby>はいつですか？　When is your birthday?

4. Why なぜ、どうして、なんで

There are a few ways to ask "why" in Japanese. The first, なぜ **(naze)**, is used in formal writing and speech but not in daily conversation. The second, どうして **(doushite)** and なんで **(nande)** are casual and are used in everyday conversation.

どうして<ruby>日本語<rt>にほんご</rt></ruby>を<ruby>勉強<rt>べんきょう</rt></ruby>しているんですか？　Why are you studying Japanese?

なんで？　Why?

5. Who だれ

The question word "who" is だれ **(dare)**. To use the possessive question word "whose," the particle の comes after the question word.

あの<ruby>人<rt>ひと</rt></ruby>は<u>だれ</u>ですか？　Who is that person?

<u>だれの</u>かさですか？　Whose umbrella is this?

6. Which どれ、どっち、どちら

When there are only two options, the question word どっち **(docchi)** or どちら **(dochira)** is used. The latter is formal. If more than two options are available, the question word どれ **(dore)** is used.

お<ruby>茶<rt>ちゃ</rt></ruby>とコーヒー、<u>どっち</u>ですか？　Which one? Tea or coffee?

<u>どれ</u>がジョンの<ruby>家<rt>いえ</rt></ruby>ですか？　Which is John's house?

7. How どう、どのように

The question word どう **(dō)** is used for asking about how things are; for example, "How was your vacation?" "How was it?" どうやって **(dōyatte)**, or どのように **(dono yōni)** is another way to express how; for example "How did you learn Japanese?" "How can I get to the station?"

<u>どう</u>だった？　How was it? (casual)

<ruby>会議<rt>かいぎ</rt></ruby>は<u>どう</u>でしたか？　How was the meeting? (formal)

<u>どうやって</u>ここに<ruby>来<rt>き</rt></ruby>たんですか？　How did you get here?

8. How many いくつ

いくつ **(ikutsu)** is a question word for asking for the quantity of something.

<ruby>卵<rt>たまご</rt></ruby>は<u>いくつ</u>ありますか？　How many eggs do you have?

9. How much (price)　いくら

The question word いくら *(ikura)* is used to ask for the price of something.

（ねだんは）いくらですか？　What is the price?

このパソコンはいくらですか？　How much is this computer?

10. How much (amount)　どのくらい

The question word どのくらい *(donokurai)* is for asking about the amount of something. It is also used to ask about the amount of time (how much time), distance (how far), and height (how tall).

東京(とうきょう)から京都(きょうと)までどのくらいで着(つ)きますか？　How long does it take from Tokyo to Kyoto?

SECTION 1-5: COUNTERS

Many languages have the concept of counters. For example, in English, we say "two slices of pizza," "three bottles of wine." Japanese has a similar concept. Different types of things, such as food servings, people, books, and so on, all use different counters. You cannot only state the numbers by themselves; rather the number and the appropriate counter are used together.

There are hundreds of counters in Japanese, but this section focuses on the most commonly used counters. Refer to the words in the box below for a list of some common counters.

Counters	People にん 人	Animals ひき 匹	Small items こ 個	Books さつ 冊
1	ひとり	いっぴき	いっこ	いっさつ
2	ふたり	にひき	にこ	にさつ
3	さんにん	さんびき	さんこ	さんさつ
4	よにん	よんひき	よんこ	よんさつ
5	ごにん	ごひき	ごこ	ごさつ
6	ろくにん	ろっぴき	ろっこ	ろくさつ
7	ななにん	ななひき	ななこ	ななさつ
8	はちにん	はっぴき	はっこ	はっさつ
9	きゅうにん	きゅうひき	きゅうこ	きゅうさつ
10	じゅうにん	じゅっぴき	じゅっこ	じゅっさつ

Counters	Cups of はい 杯	Flat things まい 枚	Long things ほん 本	Equipment だい 台	Anything つ
1	いっぱい	いちまい	いっぽん	いちだい	ひとつ
2	にはい	にまい	にほん	にだい	ふたつ
3	さんばい	さんまい	さんぼん	さんだい	みっつ
4	よんはい	よんまい	よんほん	よんだい	よっつ
5	ごはい	ごまい	ごほん	ごだい	いつつ
6	ろっぱい	ろくまい	ろっぽん	ろくだい	むっつ
7	ななはい	ななまい	ななほん	ななだい	ななつ
8	はっぱい	はちまい	はっぽん	はちだい	やっつ
9	きゅうはい	きゅうまい	きゅうほん	きゅうだい	ここのつ
10	じゅっぱい	じゅうまい	じゅっぽん	じゅうだい	（とお）

In English, numbers always come before the things you count; for example, "two people," "two bottles of wine," or "three cats." However, in Japanese, where you place the counter is fairly flexible. In the box below see the basic sentence structure for counting things.

> (things or people) が （counter words）あります / います
>
> There are…

Even though counter words are usually placed before **arimasu** or **imasu,** they also can be placed before the noun as well. See the example below.

リンゴがふたつあります。　There are two apples.

ふたつリンゴがあります。　There are two apples.

Now see how to use each counter.

1. 人: Counter for people. Note that "one person" (ひとり) and "two people" (ふたり) are irregular forms.

にほんじん　がくせい　　ふたり
日本人の学生が二人います。　There are two Japanese students.

2. 匹: Counter for small or medium-sized animals, such as dogs and cats.

犬が二匹います。　There are two dogs.
_{いぬ　にひき}

3. 個: Counter for something small, such as candy and eggs.

冷蔵庫に卵が十個あります。　There are ten eggs in the fridge.
_{れいぞうこ　たまご　じゅっこ}

4. 冊: Counter for books, magazines, and dictionaries.

つくえの上に辞書が二冊あります。　There are two dictionaries on the table.
_{うえ　じしょ　にさつ}

5. 杯: Counter for cups, glasses, and bowls; for example, two cups of coffee or three glasses of wine.

コーヒーを三杯ください。　Please give me three cups of coffee.
_{さんばい}

6. 枚: Counter for something flat, such as paper or a ticket.

チケットを二枚ください。　I would like to have two tickets.
_{にまい}

7. 本: Counter for long objects, such as pencils, umbrellas, and bottles.

玄関にかさが三本あります。　There are three umbrellas by the door.
_{げんかん　さんぼん}

8. 台: Counter for equipment, such as machines, cars, and computers.

駐車場に車が五台あります。　There are five cars in the parking lot.
_{ちゅうしゃじょう　くるま　ごだい}

9. つ: General counter used for almost anything except people and animals.

ラーメンを三つください。　Please give me three bowls of ramen.
_{みっ}

いいアイディアが一つあります。　I have a good idea.
_{ひと}

SECTION 2: VOCABULARY

Objects

かばん　bag

かさ　umbrella

とけい
時計　clock, watch

くつ　shoes

エアコン　air conditioner

パソコン　computer

つくえ　desk

ほん
本　book

じしょ
辞書　dictionary

ざっし
雑誌　magazine

チケット　ticket

かみ
紙　paper

Food

たまご
卵　egg

リンゴ　apple

コーヒー　coffee

ちゃ
お茶　tea

れいぞうこ
冷蔵庫　refrigerator

People

とも
友だち　friend

おとこ　ひと　　　だんせい
男の人 / 男性　man

おんな　ひと　　　じょせい
女の人 / 女性　woman

Animals

いぬ
犬　dog

ねこ
猫　cat

うさぎ　rabbit

ねずみ　rat, mouse

Locations

スターバックス（スタバ）　Starbucks

マクドナルド　McDonald's

レストラン　restaurant

ひ　だ
引き出し　drawer

トイレ　bathroom, toilet

げんかん
玄関　entryway

ちゅうしゃじょう
駐車場　parking lot

きょうと
京都　Kyoto

ゆうびんきょく
郵便局　post office

こうえん
公園　park

Other

じかん
時間　time

しゅみ　hobby

たんじょうび
誕生日　birthday

かいぎ
会議　meeting

ねだん
値段　price

SECTION 3: EXERCISES

SECTION 3-1: VOCABULARY

Practice 1: 単語を覚えよう
<small>たんご　おぼ</small>

Match the vocabulary that corresponds to the pictures.

① かさ　•

② <small>とけい</small>　時計　•

③ つくえ　•

④ <small>ちゅうしゃじょう</small>　駐車場　•

⑤ <small>ほん</small>　本　•

⑥ <small>れいぞうこ</small>　冷蔵庫　•

⑦ リンゴ　•

⑧ <small>たんじょうび</small>　誕生日　•

•　

•　

•　

•　

•　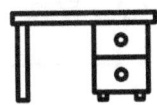

•　

•　

•

SECTION 3-2: READING AND WRITING

Practice 1: 正しい文章を選ぼう

In the pictures below, Diana and John are talking. Select the correct sentence from A to C.

①

A. これは私のかさです。

B. あれは私のかさです。

C. それは私のかさです。

②

A. これは私の本です。

B. あれは私の本です。

C. それは私の本です。

③

A. これはジョンのかばんですか？

B. それはジョンのかばんですか？

C. あれは私のかばんです。

④

A. これはジョンの自転車ですか？

B. あれはジョンの車です。

C. あれはジョンの自転車ですか？

Practice 2: 値段(ねだん)を聞(き)こう

Imagine yourself walking into a store that sells various things. You want to ask the price of each item. Choose the correct demonstrative adjectives to complete the sentences below.

① (この・その・あの) 本(ほん)はいくらですか？＿＿＿＿＿＿＿＿＿＿＿＿＿＿＿＿＿＿＿＿
② (この・その・あの) 服(ふく)はいくらですか？＿＿＿＿＿＿＿＿＿＿＿＿＿＿＿＿＿＿＿＿
③ (この・その・あの) 辞書(じしょ)はいくらですか？＿＿＿＿＿＿＿＿＿＿＿＿＿＿＿＿＿＿
④ (この・その・あの) 時計(とけい)はいくらですか？＿＿＿＿＿＿＿＿＿＿＿＿＿＿＿＿＿＿
⑤ (この・その・あの) 靴(くつ)はいくらですか？＿＿＿＿＿＿＿＿＿＿＿＿＿＿＿＿＿＿＿

Practice 3: あります or います

Choose **arimasu** or **imasu** to complete the sentence.

① 弟(おとうと)が二人(ふたり)（あります・います）。
② 学校(がっこう)にさくらの木(き)が（あります・います）。
③ 私(わたし)の家(いえ)にテレビが（あります・います）。
④ 冷蔵庫(れいぞうこ)にリンゴが（あります・います）。
⑤ 車(くるま)の上(うえ)にねこが（あります・います）。

Practice 4: 文を作ろう

Rearrange the following sentences in the correct order.

① います / が / ねこ / 駐車場 / に

_____

② トイレ / が / 紙 / ありません / に

_____

③ 友だち / アメリカ人 / の / が / います

_____

④ ねずみ / が / に / レストラン / います

_____

⑤ 本 / が / 図書館 / あります / に

_____

Practice 5: 文(ぶん)を書(か)こう

Look at Toshi's classroom below and form sentences to describe what the classroom has and what it does not have.

Example：　教(きょう)室(しつ)に黒(こく)板(ばん)があります。　There is a blackboard in the classroom.

① つくえ

_____

② 先(せんせい)生

_____

③ 花(はな)

_____

④ パソコン

_____

⑤ エアコン

_____

Practice 6: 数(かぞ)えよう

Describe each picture in Japanese with the correct counter.

Example: 女(おんな)の人(ひと)が二人(ふたり)います

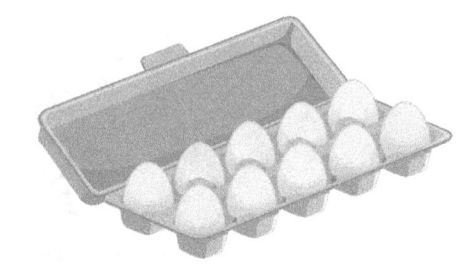

④ _____。

① _____。

⑤ _____。

② _____。

⑥ _____。

③ _____。

⑦ _____。

48　Section 3 | Lesson 2 | *Japanese Grammar Made Easy*

Practice 7: 質問に答えよう

Look at the picture and answer the questions.

① 犬はどこにいますか？

_____。

② 男の人は何人いますか？

_____。

③ 時計はどこですか？

_____。

④ パソコンはどこですか？

_____。

SECTION 3-3: LISTENING EXERCISES

 Practice 1: 私(わたし)の町(まち)

Alex is taking us on a tour of his hometown. Listen to the audio carefully. Then answer the questions from A to C.

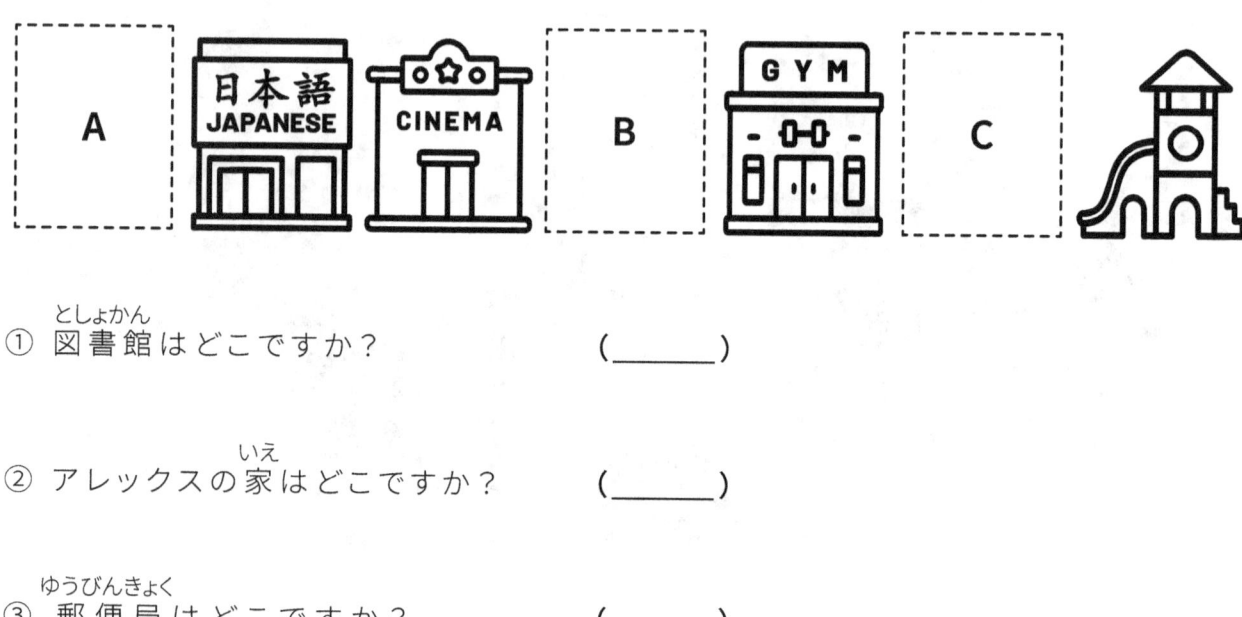

① 図書館(としょかん)はどこですか？　　　　(_____)

② アレックスの家(いえ)はどこですか？　　　(_____)

③ 郵便局(ゆうびんきょく)はどこですか？　　(_____)

Practice 2: どこですか

Alex got lost on the street. Listen to the audio recording and answer the questions.

① What Alex is looking for?

A. 日本語学校 (にほんご がっこう)

B. 図書館 (としょかん)

C. 公園 (こうえん)

D. 大学 (だいがく)

② Where is the park? Write the answer in Japanese.

_____

③ Where is the Japanese school? Write the answer in Japanese.

_____

第三章
だいさんしょう
LESSON 3

ADJECTIVES

もくひょう 目標 OBJECTIVE

✓ Learn how to conjugate い-adjectives and な-adjectives.
✓ Learn how to form sentences using various adjectives.

ないよう 内容 CONTENTS

Section 1: Grammar
Section 1-1: Adjectives
Section 1-2: Like and Dislikes
Section 1-3: How To Describe Appearance
Section 1-4: Te-form of Adjectives
Section 1-5: Adjective + なる
Section 2: Vocabulary
Section 3: Exercises

SECTION 1: GRAMMAR

SECTION 1-1: ADJECTIVES

Adjectives are words that describe a noun; for example, "beautiful," "big," and "expensive." All adjectives in Japanese fall under one of two groups. The first group is called い-adjectives and the second group is called な-adjectives. These two groups of adjectives follow different conjugation patterns. Unlike in English, you also need to conjugate adjectives depending on the tense, whether it be present or past tense.

Group 1: い-adjective

All い-adjectives end with the hiragana character い. See some examples of い-adjectives.

<ruby>面<rt>おもしろ</rt></ruby>白い   interesting, funny

<ruby>大<rt>おお</rt></ruby>きい   big

<ruby>暑<rt>あつ</rt></ruby>い   hot

<ruby>忙<rt>いそが</rt></ruby>しい   busy

Just as in English, an adjective in Japanese modifies the noun that immediately follows it.

<ruby>面<rt>おもしろ</rt></ruby>白い<ruby>映画<rt>えいが</rt></ruby>   an interesting movie

<ruby>大<rt>おお</rt></ruby>きい<ruby>車<rt>くるま</rt></ruby>   a big car

When the adjective comes at the end of a sentence—such as "This car is big" or "Today is busy"—it must be conjugated accordingly. The examples below show how to conjugate い-adjectives.

Plain form	Present		Past	
	Affirmative	Negative	Affirmative	Negative
大きい big	大きい	大きくない	大きかった	大きくなかった

To sound more polite, add the auxiliary verb です **(desu)** after these adjectives (affirmative and negative).

Examples:

ジョンの家は大きいです。 John's house is big.

ジョンの家は大きくないです。 John's house is not big.

> ### Basic Conjugation Rules of the い- adjectives
> · Replace い with くない for the negative present tense form
> · Replace い with かった for the affirmative past tense form
> · Replace い with くなかった for the negative past tense form

There is only one important exception. Please note below.

Plain form	Present		Past	
	Affirmative	Negative	Affirmative	Negative
いい *good*	いい	よくない	よかった	よくなかった

Another adjective that conjugates like this is かっこいい **(kakkoii)**, which means handsome or cool. If you look closely at this adjective, you can see the いい ending, indicating it follows the same い-adjective conjugation pattern.

Examples:

とてもいい映画でした。 It was a really nice movie.

体調がよくないです。 I don't feel well.

ジョンはかっこよかった！ John looked good!

Group 2: な-adjective

All な-adjectives end with the hiragana character な. See some examples of な-adjectives.

<ruby>元気<rt>げんき</rt></ruby>な healthy, active

きれいな beautiful

しずかな quiet

ひまな not busy, bored

Just the same as the い-adjective, な-adjectives modify the noun that follows it.

<ruby>元気<rt>げんき</rt></ruby>な<ruby>男<rt>おとこ</rt></ruby>の<ruby>子<rt>こ</rt></ruby> an active boy

きれいな<ruby>公園<rt>こうえん</rt></ruby> a beautiful park

な-adjectives act essentially like nouns. All the conjugation rules for both nouns and な-adjectives are the same.

Plain form	Present		Past	
	Affirmative	Negative	Affirmative	Negative
きれいな *beautiful*	きれい	きれいじゃない	きれいだった	きれいじゃなかった

Just as with い-adjectives, the auxiliary verb です *(desu)* can be added to sound more polite in the present affirmative, present negative, and past negative form. But for the past tense affirmative form, だった *(datta)* can be replaced with でした *(deshita)* to be polite.

Example:

この<ruby>公園<rt>こうえん</rt></ruby>はきれいです。 This park is beautiful.

<ruby>日本<rt>にほん</rt></ruby>の<ruby>桜<rt>さくら</rt></ruby>はきれいでした。 The Japanese cherry blossoms were beautiful.

> **Basic Conjugation Rules of the な-adjectives**
> · For the affirmative present form, replace な with だ
> · For the negative present form, replace な with じゃない
> · For the affirmative past form, replace な with だった
> · For the negative past form, replace な with じゃなかった

How do you say "I'm hungry" or "I'm thirsty" in Japanese? The equivalent words for "hungry" or "thirsty" in Japanese are not adjectives. See the sentence below.

おなかがすいた   I'm hungry

のどがかわいた   I'm thirsty

In the first sentence, **onaka** means "stomach" and **suita** means "empty." Therefore, the literal translation is "stomach has become empty."

In the second sentence, **nodo** means "throat" and **kawaita** means "dry." The literal translation is "throat has become dry."

SECTION 1-2: LIKES AND DISLIKES

In this section, you will learn how to express your likes and dislikes in Japanese. Two な-adjectives are used to express what you like and what you don't like.

好きな   like, favorite, desirable

嫌いな   dislike, disgusted with

In English, "like" and "dislike" are verbs. However, in Japanese, **sukina** and **kiraina** are adjectives, therefore their conjugation patterns are just like な-adjectives.

	Present		Past	
	Affirmative	Negative	Affirmative	Negative
好<ruby>き</ruby> *like*	好き	好きじゃない	好きだった	好きじゃなかった
嫌い *dislike*	嫌い	嫌いじゃない	嫌いだった	嫌いじゃなかった

Follow the grammar pattern below to express your likes and dislikes.

〜が好き（です）。 I like ...

〜が好きじゃない（です）。 I don't like...

Example:

好きな食べ物は何ですか？ What is your favorite food?

（私は）ラーメンが好きです。 I like ramen.

コーヒーは好きじゃないです。 I don't like coffee.

なっとうは嫌いです。 I dislike natto beans.

If you really like something, you can use 大好き *(daisuki)* instead of **suki** to intensify the feeling conveyed. If you don't like something, you can use **suki janai**. However, if you want to take it a step further and say you hate something, you can use **kirai** instead of **suki janai**.

58 Section 1 | Lesson 3 | *Japanese Grammar Made Easy*

When someone asks you if you like a specific thing, and if you neither like nor dislike something, you can use the expression below.

好きでも嫌いでもないです。   I neither like nor dislike it.

SECTION 1-3: HOW TO DESCRIBE APPEARANCE

To describe the appearance of someone, follow the sentence structure below.

> (name of the person) は (body parts) が (adjective) です。

Example:

サンディは目が大きいです。   Sandy has big eyes.

スカイは目が悪いです。   Sky has bad eyesight.

ジョンは背が高いです。   John is tall.

フアンは背が低いです。   Juan is short.

Extra Point

Below are other useful phrases to describe appearance. In any culture, discussing people's appearance can be a delicate and sensitive subject. However, in some cases, we may genuinely need to describe what someone looks like and so the need for this vocabulary arises.

太っています： fat, overweight

トシ先生はちょっと太っています。   Teacher Toshi is a little overweight.

やせています： skinny, slim

フアンはやせています。   Juan is skinny.

The equivalent words for English "thin" or "fat" are not adjectives in Japanese, but they are te-forms of verbs. You will learn about te-form verbs in Lesson 5.

SECTION 1-4: *TE*-FORM OF ADJECTIVES

If you want to use more than two adjectives in one sentence, for example, "The hotel was cheap and clean," "Tokyo is big and lively," the *te*-form is used for the first adjective in the sentence. Below see how to make *te*-form of adjectives.

	adjective	*te*-form
い-adjective	大(おお)きい	大(おお)き<u>くて</u>
irregular	いい	<u>よくて</u>
な-adjective	元気(げんき)な	元気(げんき)<u>で</u>

To form *te*-form of い-adjective, replace い with くて. The *te*-form of な-adjective is formed by replacing な with で.

Example:

ホテルは安(やす)<u>くて</u>きれいでした。 The hotel was inexpensive and beautiful.

東京(とうきょう)は大(おお)<u>きくて</u>にぎやかです。 Tokyo is big and lively.

サンディは頭(あたま)が<u>よくて</u>きれいです。 Sandy is smart and beautiful.

SECTION 1-5: ADJECTIVE + なる

The verb なる *(naru)* is a very useful verb that is used to indicate change. It is often used with both groups of adjectives and nouns.

To become: なる		
い-adjectives	寒い (さむ) cold	寒くなる (さむ) to get cold
な-adjectives	元気な (げんき) healthy	元気になる (げんき) to feel better
nouns	医者 (いしゃ) doctor	医者になる (いしゃ) to become a doctor

The particle に should be used after the noun. For い-adjectives, the final い is replaced with **kunaru**. For な-adjectives, the final な is replaced with **ni naru.** The examples below illustrate this.

Example:

だんだん寒くなりました。 It gradually became cold.

サンディは日本語が上手になりました。 Sandy has become better at speaking Japanese.

ディアナは医者になりました。 Diana became a doctor.

SECTION 2: VOCABULARY

い-adjectives

おもしろ
面白い　amusing, interesting

おお
大きい　big

ちい
小さい　small

なが
長い　long

みじか
短い　short

かわいい　cute, adorable

あつ
暑い　hot

さむ
寒い　cold

いそが
忙しい　busy

ひろ
広い　spacious

せま
狭い　narrow

いい　good

わる
悪い　bad

やす
安い　inexpensive

たか
高い　expensive, high

おいしい　delicious

あたら
新しい　new

ふる
古い　old

むずか
難しい　difficult

な-adjectives

げんき
元気な　healthy, active

きれいな　beautiful

しずかな　quiet

ひまな
す
好きな　like, favorite

きら
嫌いな　dislike

あんぜん
安全な　safe

きけん
危険な　dangerous

かんたん
簡単な　easy

たいせつ
大切な　important

まじめ
真面目な　serious

ふくざつ
複雑な　complicated

しんせつ
親切な　kind

じょうず
上手な　skillful, good

にぎやかな　lively

Body parts

あたま
頭　head

みみ
耳　ear

め
目　eye

くち
口　mouth

あし
足　foot

かみ
髪　hair

かお
顔　face

からだ
体　body

ちから
力　power, strength

たいちょう
体調　physical condition

People

おとこ　こ
男の子　boy

おんな　こ
女の子　girl

Hobbies

おんがく
音楽　music

えいが
映画　movie

りょうり
料理　cooking

しゃしん
写真　picture

りょこう
旅行　traveling

スポーツ　sport

Locations

ぎんこう
銀行　bank

にわ
庭　garden

みち
道　street

SECTION 3: EXERCISES

SECTION 3-1: VOCABULARY

Practice 1: 単語を覚えよう
<small>たんご　おぼ</small>

Match the vocabulary that corresponds to the pictures.

① 忙しい ●
<small>いそが</small>

② 暑い ●
<small>あつ</small>

③ 元気な ●
<small>げんき</small>

④ 危険な ●
<small>きけん</small>

⑤ 背が高い ●
<small>せ　たか</small>

⑥ 頭がいい ●
<small>あたま</small>

⑦ ひまな ●

⑧ 安い ●
<small>やす</small>

SECTION 3-2: READING AND WRITING

Practice 1: 形容詞(けいようし)

Complete the conjugation table below by filling in the appropriate forms for each adjective. Inside the parentheses, provide the English translation of each adjective.

① い-adjectives

Plain form	Present		Past	
	Affirmative	Negative	Affirmative	Negative
おもしろい ( )				
ちいさい ( )				
ながい ( )				
みじかい ( )				
あつい ( )				
さむい ( )				
いそがしい ( )				
ひろい ( )				
せまい ( )				
わるい ( )				
やすい ( )				
たかい ( )				
おいしい ( )				
あたらしい ( )				
むずかしい ( )				

② な-adjectives

Plain form	Present		Past	
	Affirmative	Negative	Affirmative	Negative
げんきな ( )				
しずかな ( )				
ひまな ( )				
あんぜんな ( )				
きけんな ( )				
かんたんな ( )				
たいせつな ( )				
まじめな ( )				
ふくざつな ( )				
しんせつな ( )				

Practice 2: 空白(くうはく)をうめよう

① It's hot today.

今日(きょう)は _____ です。

② Japanese is not difficult.

日本語(にほんご)は _____ です。

③ This watch is expensive.

この時計(とけい)は _____ です。

④ The test was difficult.

テストは _____ です。

⑤ This pizza is not delicious.

このピザは＿＿＿＿＿＿＿＿＿＿です。

⑥ John's house is big.

ジョンの家は＿＿＿＿＿＿＿＿＿＿です。

⑦ This city isn't safe.

この街_{まち}は＿＿＿＿＿＿＿＿＿＿です。

Practice 3: どんな車_{くるま}

Examine the following pictures and describe them using adjectives.

Example: たかいくるまです。

①_____

②_____

③_____

④_____

⑤_____

66 Section 3 | Lesson 3 | Japanese Grammar Made Easy

Practice 4: 質問に答えよう
<small>しつもん こた</small>

Answer the questions below.

① 日本語は簡単ですか？
<small>にほんご　かんたん</small>

_____

② 今日はひまですか？
<small>きょう</small>

_____

③ 日本の食べ物はおいしいですか？
<small>にほん　た　もの</small>

_____

④ 今日は暑いですか？
<small>きょう　あつ</small>

_____

⑤ 学校の先生はやさしいですか？
<small>がっこう　せんせい</small>

_____

Practice 5: 過去形
<small>かこけい</small>

Translate following sentences into Japanese.

① My room was clean yesterday.

_____

② The weather wasn't good today.

_____

③ The movie wasn't interesting.

_____

④ There was an important test.

_____

⑤ The shoes were inexpensive.

_____

⑥ My younger sister was short.

_____

⑦ My older sister had long hair.

_____

⑧ I had some free time yesterday.

_____

⑨ The parking lot is spacious.

_____

⑩ This Japanese dictionary wasn't expensive.

_____

Practice 6: 人の見た目

Describe the appearance of Sky and Noa in Japanese.

スカイ

① 目_____

② 脚_____

③ 髪_____

ノア

① 脚_____

② 体_____

③ 髪_____

Practice 7: 好き嫌い

Answer the questions based on your personal preferences using すき or きらい.

Example:

Question: ラーメンは好きですか？　　　Do you like ramen noodles?

Answer: いいえ、好きじゃないです。　　No, I don't like ramen noodles.

① すしは好きですか？
_____

② バスケットボールは好きですか？
_____

③ 日本の音楽は好きですか？
_____

④ 映画は好きですか？
_____

⑤ アニメは好きですか？
_____

⑥ 犬は好きですか？
_____

⑦ パソコンは好きですか？
_____

⑧ 旅行は好きですか？
_____

Practice 8: どんな人

Describe each person using two adjectives.

① サンディ	② ディアナ	③ ジョン	④ アレックス	⑤ トシ
active and cute	quiet and smart	funny and tall	kind and serious	smart and kind

① サンディ

_____

② ディアナ

_____

③ ジョン

_____

④ アレックス

_____

⑤ トシ

_____

SECTION 3-3: LISTENING EXERCISES

 Practice 1: 私の家
わたし いえ

Alex explains what his house looks like. Listen to the audio recording and choose the correct answer from A to D.

① アレックスの家
いえ

A. おおきい　　B. ちいさい　　C. ふるい　　D. たかい

② 庭
にわ

A. せまい　　B. あたらしい　　C. ひろい　　D. きたない

③ テレビ

A. やすい　　B. たかい　　C. ひろい　　D. おおきい

 Practice 2: 何が好き
なに す

Diana is explaining what she likes. Listen to the audio recording and answer the questions.

① サンディはカレーライスが好きですか？
　　　　　　　　　　　　　　す

_____

② サンディはバスケットボールが好きですか？
　　　　　　　　　　　　　　　　　す

_____

Practice 3: どんな犬(いぬ)

Toshi was walking with his dog and he met Diana. Listen to the recording and indicate if the sentences are true or false.

① ペコは大(おお)きくて力(ちから)が強(つよ)いです。　(True/False)

② ペコは耳(みみ)が大(おお)きいです。　(True/False)

③ サミーは力(ちから)が強(つよ)くてやさしいです。　(True/False)

Practice 4: 旅行(りょこう)はどうだった？

Sandy just got back from Kozushima island in Tokyo. She explains how her vacation was. Listen to the audio recording and describe how each activity was.

① ビーチ

_____

② ホテル

_____

③ サーフィン

_____

第四章
だいよんしょう
LESSON 4

VERBS AND PARTICLES

目標 (もくひょう) OBJECTIVE

√ Learn the sentence order in Japanese.
√ Learn how to make affirmative and negative forms of verbs.
√ Learn how to change verbs into the past tense.
√ Learn the function of each particle.

内容 (ないよう) CONTENTS

Section 1: Grammar

Section 1-1: Verbs in Japanese

Section 1-2: Sentence Structure in Japanese

Section 1-3: Present Tense

Section 1-4: Frequency Adverbs

Section 1-5: Past Tense

Section 1-6: Particles in Japanese

Section 2: Vocabulary

Section 3: Exercises

SECTION 1: GRAMMAR

SECTION 1-1: VERBS IN JAPANESE

A verb is used to refer to actions and to express state-of-being. Some examples of verbs are speak, write, walk, and eat. In English, verbs change based on who is speaking; for example, "I eat" and "he eats." However, in Japanese, verbs remain the same regardless of who the speaker is.

Below is a list of verbs translated into Japanese.

た
食べる　eat

い
行く　go

か
書く　write

はな
話す　speak

SECTION 1-2: SENTENCE STRUCTURE IN JAPANESE

The sentence structure in Japanese is quite different from English. English is a Subject-Verb-Object (SVO) language. On the other hand, Japanese is a Subject-Object-Verb (SOV) language. However, the word order in Japanese is quite flexible. Sometimes, the subject can also appear after the object. A good rule to remember in Japanese is that the verb always goes at the end. See below an example of the basic sentence structure in Japanese.

> **Sentence structure: Subject + Object + Verb**
>
> た
> Example:わたしはピザを食べます。
>
> I eat pizza.

Unlike English, personal pronouns are often omitted unless you want to make it clear who does it. Also, the object can be omitted as well if it is clear from the context. See the example sentence below.

た
ピザを食べますか？　Are you going to eat some pizza?

た
はい、食べます。　Yes, I'm going to eat it.

In both sentences above, personal pronouns such as **watashi** or **anata** are omitted because it is clear from the context.

SECTION 1-3: PRESENT TENSE

There are three types of verbs in Japanese, which will allow us to define the conjugation rule. The first group of verbs is called *ru*-verbs. The second group is called *u*-verbs. The third group is called irregular verbs. In this lesson, we will learn the three forms of verbs. First, the dictionary form or plain form. Second, the present tense affirmative forms; and finally, present tense negative forms.

Another factor that is worth remembering is that the "present tense" you learn in this section can be used for (1) the activities in which a person habitually or regularly engages and (2) the activities that a person will do in the future. Therefore the "present tense" of the verbs here is not only used for the present tense but also for the future tense.

1) Group 1: *ru*-verb

All the *ru*-verbs end with the hiragana character: る (*ru*). See the examples of *ru*-verbs provided below.

た
食べる *to eat*

き
着る *to put on*

ね
寝る *to go to sleep*

お
起きる *to get up*

For the present tense affirmative form, replace final **ru** with **masu**. For the present tense negative form, replace final **ru** with **masen**. See the box below.

Note that the forms using ます and ません are used in polite speech. For casual or informal situations, different verb endings are used, which will be covered later.

Plain Form	Affirmative	Negative
た 食べる *to eat*	た 食べます	た 食べません
tabe**ru**	tabe**masu**	tabe**masen**

Summary

- For the affirmative form, replace る(*ru*) with ます (*masu*).
- For the negative form, replace る(*ru*) with ません (*masen*).

2) Group 2: *u*-verb

U-verbs end with the romaji *u* sound. If a verb does not end in る (*ru*), it is always a *u*-verb. However, some *u*-verbs do end in る, which can be confusing. A common rule is that if the syllable before る contains the vowel *i* or *e*, the verb is most likely a *ru*-verb. If it contains *a*, *u*, or *o*, it is usually a *u*-verb. However, there are many exceptions. For example, *hairu* (to enter) and *hashiru* (to run) have *i* before *ru*, but they are *u*-verbs. Because of these exceptions, it's helpful to learn each verb's group individually.

The example below illustrates how to conjugate *u*-verbs.

Plain Form	Affirmative	Negative
のむ to drink	のみます	のみません
no**mu**	nomi**masu**	nomi**masen**

Here are some examples of *u*-verbs that end with る (*ru*).

はい 入る	to enter	し 知る	to know
はし 走る	to run	かえ 帰る	to return
いる	to need	しゃべる	to chat
き 切る	to cut	つく 作る	to make

Summary

- For the affirmative, replace ***u*** with ***imasu***.
- For the negative form, replace ***u*** with ***imasen***.

3) Group 3: irregular verb

There are only two irregular verbs. They do not follow the conjugation patterns in group 1 or group 2, as discussed above.

Plain Form	Affirmative	Negative
する *to do*	します	しません
suru	shimasu	shimasen
くる *to come*	きます	きません
kuru	kimasu	kimasen

SECTION 1-4: FREQUENCY ADVERBS

Frequency adverbs describe how often you do something; for example, "often" or "sometimes" in English. See the list and example sentences below.

Frequency adverbs	meaning	Frequency adverbs	meaning
まいにち 毎日	every day	ときどき	sometimes
いつも	always	たまに	occasionally
よく	often	あまり	not often
たいてい	usually	ぜんぜん、まったく	never, not at all

The location of frequency adverbs in the sentence is flexible. Also, note that あまり (**amari**) and ぜんぜん (**zenzen**) are always used with negative form of verbs.

Example:

私は毎日コーヒーを飲みます。   I drink coffee *every day*.

たまにジムに行きます。   I go to the gym *sometimes*.

ジョンは<u>あまり</u>勉強<u>しません</u>。　　　John *doesn't* study *much*.

スカイは<u>ぜんぜん</u>お酒を飲<u>みません</u>。　　Sky *doesn't* drink alcohol *at all*.

Extra Point

Grammatically, Japanese verbs always contain two parts: the verb base and a suffix. The *ru*-verbs always start with the base and end with the suffix **ru**. The *u*-verbs start with the verb base and end with the suffix **u**.

食べる (***taberu***) = a verb base: ***tabe*** + a suffix: ***ru***

飲む (***nomu***) = a verb base: ***nom*** + a suffix: ***u***

The part that comes before ます (***masu***) in affirmative form of verbs is called the "stem."

<u>食べ</u>ます ＝ stem: たべ＋ます

<u>飲み</u>ます ＝ stem: のみ＋ます

SECTION 1-5: PAST TENSE

In this section, we will learn how to form the past tense. For the past-tense affirmative forms of verbs, replace ます (***masu***) with ました (***mashita***). For the negative form, でした (***deshita***) will be added after ません (***masen***).

See the examples below.

	Affirmative		Negative	
	Present	Past	Present	Past
ru-verb	たべます	たべ<u>ました</u>	たべません	たべません<u>でした</u>
u-verb	のみます	のみ<u>ました</u>	のみません	のみません<u>でした</u>
Irregular verb	します	し<u>ました</u>	しません	しません<u>でした</u>
	きます	き<u>ました</u>	きません	きません<u>でした</u>

SECTION 1-6: PARTICLES IN JAPANESE

Nouns in sentences are followed by one or two hiragana characters called the "particle." Each particle indicates how the word before it relates to other words in the sentence, usually to the verb.

Purpose	Particle
Topic	は
Emphasis	が
Direct object	を
Location and means	で
Time and goal of movement	に
Goal of movement	へ
Origin	から
Co-participant	と

(All particles connect to → Verb)

- は: **Topic particle**

This particle is written in hiragana は (**ha**). When it is used as a particle, it is pronounced **"wa"**. It comes after the topic of a sentence. It can be translated as "as for" or "speaking of" in English. See the examples below.

Example:

私<u>は</u>図書館に行きます。　　I am going to the library.
(わたし　としょかん)

今日<u>は</u>雨です。　　As for today, it's rainy.
(きょう　あめ)

- が: **Emphasis**

The particle が often indicates and emphasizes the subject of the sentence. It is also used when the subject gives the listener new information. Therefore, question words such as 何 (what), だれ (who), and どこ (where) are subjects; they usually go with this particle.

だれが日本語を話せますか？　　Who speaks Japanese?

ジョンさんが（日本語を）話せます。　　John speaks Japanese.

In the example above, the name John is emphasized by using the particle が.

- **を: Object particle**

The object particle usually comes after the direct object of an action. See the examples below.

Example:

テレビを見ます。　　I am going to watch TV.

コーヒーを飲みます。　　I drink coffee.

- **で: Location and means particle**

The particle で indicates location. It can be translated as "in" or "at" in English. This particle is also used to indicate the means by which something is done. It can be translated as "by" or "with" in English.

Example:

家で映画を見ます。　　I am going to watch a movie at home. (*location*)

車でシカゴに行きます。　　I am going to Chicago by car. (*means*)

- **に: Goal of movement and time**

This particle has multiple functions. It is mainly used to indicate time or movement. This particle can also be used to indicate location, just as the particle で. What is the difference between the particle で and the particle に? While で tends to indicate the location where action or events take place, に indicates the location where something or someone exists. The particle に is used with verbs such as いる ("to be" for people, animals), ある ("to be" for nonliving things), すむ (to live), とまる (to stay).

Example:

サンディは東京に住んでいます。　　Sandy lives <u>in Tokyo</u>. (*location*)

ホテルに泊まりました。　　I stayed <u>in the hotel</u>. (*location*)

明日、学校に行きます。　　I'm going <u>to school</u> tomorrow. (*goal of movement*)

日曜日に映画を見ます。　　I'm going to watch a movie <u>on Sunday</u>. (*time*)

１時にお昼ごはんを食べました。　　I ate lunch <u>at 1</u>. (*time*)

- **へ: Goal of movement**

The particle へ also indicates the goal of movement. When the hiragana character へ is used as a particle, it is pronounced as "e."

Example:

明日、学校へ行きます。　　I'm going <u>to school</u> tomorrow. (*goal of movement*)

- **から: Origin**

The particle から indicates the starting point of something or from where something comes.

Example:

８時から働きます。　　I work <u>from</u> 8 o'clock.

カナダから来ました。　　I am <u>from</u> Canada.

- **と: Co-participant**

The particle と mainly has two functions. First, it can be used to connect two nouns. In English. it is similar to the joining word "and." Second, it is used to describe with whom you do something.

Example:

ディアナは英語とスペイン語を話します。　　Diana speaks English <u>and</u> Spanish.

すしと天ぷらを食べました。　　I ate sushi <u>and</u> tempura.

友だちと沖縄に行きました。　　I went to Okinawa <u>with</u> my friend.

SECTION 2: VOCABULARY

Ru-verbs
た
食べる　to eat
み
見る　to see
ね
寝る　to sleep
お
起きる　to wake, to occur
かんが
考える　to think
おし
教える　to teach, to inform
で
出かける　to go out
き
着る　to wear
あ
開ける　to open
し
閉める　to close
お
降りる　to get off

U-verbs
はな
話す　to speak
い
行く　to go
き
聞く　to ask, to listen
ひ
弾く　to play (musical instrument)
およ
泳ぐ　to swim
あそ
遊ぶ　to play, hang out, spend time
ま
待つ　to wait
の
飲む　to drink
よ
読む　to read
か
買う　to buy

はい
入る　to enter
はし
走る　to run

いる　to need
き
切る　to cut
かえ
帰る　to return

しゃべる　to chat
つく
作る　to make

Irregular verbs

する　to do, to play (games, sports)

くる　to come
べんきょう
勉強する　to study

そうじする　to clean

Days of the week
げつようび
月曜日　Monday
かようび
火曜日　Tuesday
すいようび
水曜日　Wednesday
もくようび
木曜日　Thursday
きんようび
金曜日　Friday
どようび
土曜日　Saturday
にちようび
日曜日　Sunday

Objects
しんかんせん
新幹線　bullet train (Shinkansen)

<ruby>自転車<rt>じてんしゃ</rt></ruby>　bicycle
<ruby>お酒<rt>さけ</rt></ruby>　alcohol
<ruby>着物<rt>きもの</rt></ruby>　kimono (Japanese traditional dress)

Locations

<ruby>教会<rt>きょうかい</rt></ruby>　church
<ruby>お寺<rt>てら</rt></ruby>　temple
<ruby>建物<rt>たてもの</rt></ruby>　building

Languages

スペイン<ruby>語<rt>ご</rt></ruby>　Spanish
<ruby>英語<rt>えいご</rt></ruby>　English
<ruby>外国語<rt>がいこくご</rt></ruby>　foreign language

SECTION 3: EXERCISES

SECTION 3-1: VOCABULARY

Practice 1: 単語を覚えよう

Match the vocabulary that corresponds to the pictures.

① 食べる • •

② 作る • •

③ 話す • •

④ 読む • •

⑤ 聞く • •

⑥ 見る • •

⑦ 飲む • •

⑧ 起きる • •

SECTION 3-2: READING AND WRITING

Practice 1: 動詞(どうし)

Below is a table of conjugation of verbs. Carefully review it and complete the blank spaces.

① *ru*-verbs

Dictionary form	Affirmative	Negative
Example: たべる　to eat	たべます	たべません
きる		
ねる		
おきる		
でかける		
みる		
おしえる		
あける		
しめる		

② *u*-verbs

Dictionary form	Affirmative	Negative
はなす		
きく		
ひく		
およぐ		
あそぶ		
のむ		
よむ		
かう		
いる		

Practice 2: 文を読もう

Choose the correct translation of the Japanese sentences below, from A to D.

① うどんを食べます。

A. I'm going to eat *Udon*.
B. I'm going to buy some *Udon*.
C. I don't eat *Udon*.
D. I won't buy *Udon*.

② 友だちとテレビを見ます。

A. I'm going to watch a movie at home.
B. I'm going to talk to my friend.
C. I'm going to hang out with my friend.
D. I'm going to watch TV with my friend.

③ ディアナはスペイン語を話します。

A. Diana speaks English.
B. Diana is going to Spain.
C. Diana speaks Spanish.
D. Diana doesn't speak Spanish.

④ 日曜日に友だちと出かけます。

A. I'm going out with my family on Sunday.
B. I'm going to my friend's house on Sunday.
C. I'm going to go out with my friend on Sunday.
D. I'm going to talk to my friend on Sunday.

⑤ 朝ごはんを作ります。

A. I'm going to make breakfast.
B. I'm going to eat breakfast.
C. I won't eat breakfast.
D. I'm going to buy some breakfast.

Practice 3: スケジュール

Sandy made a weekly schedule. Read the schedule and write what she is going to do each day.

Day	Activity
Sunday	Shopping with friends
Monday	Studying at a coffee shop
Tuesday	Going to the bank
Wednesday	Talking with my family
Thursday	Cleaning the house
Friday	Going to the restaurant with my husband*
Saturday	Relaxing and watching movies at home

*husband: おっと

Example: 火曜日(かようび)

<u>かようびにぎんこうにいきます。</u>

① 日曜日 (にちようび)

_____

② 月曜日 (げつようび)

_____

③ 水曜日 (すいようび)

_____

④ 木曜日 (もくようび)

_____

⑤ 金曜日 (きんようび)

_____

⑥ 土曜日 (どようび)

_____

Practice 4: 文(ぶん)を書(か)こう

Translate the following sentences into Japanese.

① I listen to Japanese music.

_____

② I'm going swimming this Saturday.

_____

③ I'm going to make dinner tonight.

_____

④ I'm going to get up at 6.

_____

⑤ Sandy speaks Japanese at home.

_____

⑥ Toshi doesn't speak Spanish.

_____

⑦ Alex goes to Starbucks on Wednesday.

_____

⑧ John goes to sleep at 11 p.m.

_____

⑨ Diana doesn't eat hamburgers.

___

⑩ Noa doesn't play the piano.

___

Practice 5: 質問(しつもん)に答(こた)えよう

Answer the following questions using the frequency adverbs below.

毎日(まいにち)	たいてい	あまり
いつも	ときどき	ぜんぜん
よく	たまに	

① 日本(にほん)のアニメを見(み)ますか？

___

② 日本(にほん)の映画(えいが)を見(み)ますか？

___

③ 朝(あさ)ごはんを食(た)べますか？

___

④ コーヒーを飲(の)みますか？

___

⑤ お酒(さけ)を飲(の)みますか？

___

⑥ 車(くるま)を運転(うんてん)しますか？

_____

⑦ 教会(きょうかい)に行(い)きますか？

_____

⑧ マンガを読(よ)みますか？

_____

Practice 6: 過去形(かこけい)

Below is a table of the conjugation of verbs. Please review it carefully and fill in the missing sections.

① *ru*-verbs

Dictionary form	Past tense affirmative	Past tense negative
Example: たべる	たべました	たべませんでした
きる		
ねる		
おきる		
でかける		
みる		
おしえる		
あける		
しめる		

② *u*-verbs

Dictionary form	Past tense affirmative	Past tense negative
はなす		
きく		
ひく		
およぐ		
あそぶ		
のむ		
よむ		
かえる		
しゃべる		

Practice 7: 空白をうめよう

Fill in the blank spaces with the correct particle.

① わたし_____中学生です。　I am a junior high school student.

② わたし_____父_____６０才です。　My father is 60 years old.

③ 図書館_____行きます。I'm going to the library.

④ 図書館_____本_____読みました。　I read a book at the library.

⑤ 友だちの家_____映画_____見ました。　I watched a movie at my friend's house.

⑥ わたしはお茶_____飲みます。　I'm going to drink tea.

⑦ 自転車_____郵便局_____行きます。　I'm going to the post office by bike.

⑧ 新幹線_____大阪_____行きます。　I'm going to Osaka by Shinkansen.

⑨ ７時_____夜ごはん_____食べます。I'm going to eat dinner at 7 o'clock.

⑩ 友だち_____サッカー_____します。I'm going to play soccer with my friends.

⑪ 新しい服_____くつ_____買いました。　I bought new clothes and shoes.

⑫ タコス_____サラダ_____食べました。　I ate tacos and a salad.

⑬ 友だちの家_____泊まりました。　I stayed at my friend's house.

⑭ シカゴ_____来ました。I came from Chicago.

⑮ 集会_____１０時_____始まります。The meeting starts at 10 o'clock.

Practice 8: 日記(にっき)を読(よ)もう

Alex went to Japan during his summer vacation. Read his diary below and answer the questions that follow.

August 7th 2022

夏休(なつやす)みに日本(にほん)に行(い)きました。まず東京(とうきょう)に行(い)きました。東京(とうきょう)でスカイツリーと浅草寺(せんそうじ)を見(み)ました。浅草寺(せんそうじ)は古(ふる)いお寺(てら)です。それから渋谷(しぶや)でお寿司(すし)を食(た)べました。そのあと新幹線(しんかんせん)で京都(きょうと)へ行(い)きました。古(ふる)いお寺や建物(たてもの)を見(み)ました。着物(きもの)を着(き)て写真(しゃしん)をとりました。おみやげをたくさん買(か)いました。それから電車(でんしゃ)で大阪(おおさか)に行(い)きました。大阪(おおさか)は大(おお)きな街(まち)でした。大阪(おおさか)でたこ焼(や)きを食(た)べました。とてもおいしかったです。

Question 1: Choose the correct order of his trip in Japan from A to C.

A: 東京(とうきょう) → 大阪(おおさか) → 京都(きょうと)

B: 大阪(おおさか) → 東京(とうきょう) → 京都(きょうと)

C: 東京(とうきょう) → 京都(きょうと) → 大阪(おおさか)

Question 2: Where did Alex eat sushi?
A: お寺(てら)　　　B: 渋谷(しぶや)　　　C: 京都(きょうと)　　　D: スカイツリー

Question 3: What form of public transportation did he use to go to Kyoto?
A: 電車(でんしゃ)　　　B: 自転車(じてんしゃ)　　　C: 車(くるま)　　　D: 新幹線(しんかんせん)

Question 4: What form of public transportation did he use to go to Osaka?
A: 電車(でんしゃ)　　　B: 自転車(じてんしゃ)　　　C: 車(くるま)　　　D: 新幹線(しんかんせん)

SECTION 3-3: LISTENING EXERCISES

 Practice 1: 今週(こんしゅう)は何(なに)をしましたか？

Toshi, Sandy, Diana, and Alex explain what they did this week. Listen to the audio recording and answer the questions in Japanese.

① トシ

Question 1: 水曜日(すいようび)は何(なに)をしましたか？

_____

Question 2: いつレストランに行(い)きましたか？

_____

② サンディ

Question 1: 土曜日(どようび)は何(なに)をしましたか？

_____

Question 2: いつ仕事(しごと)をしましたか？

_____

③ アレックス

Question 1: 金曜日(きんようび)は何(なに)をしましたか？

_____

Question 2: いつ教会(きょうかい)に行(い)きましたか？

_____

④ ディアナ

Question 1: 月曜日(げつようび)は何(なに)をしましたか？

_____

Question 2: いつジムに行(い)きましたか？

_____

Practice 2: 今日(きょう)は何(なに)をしますか？

John explains what he is going to do today. Listen to the audio recording and answer the questions.

Question 1: 何時(なんじ)から仕事(しごと)をしますか？

___

Question 2: 何時(なんじ)に家(いえ)に帰(かえ)りますか？

___

Question 3: 7時(じ)に何(なに)をしますか？

___

Question 4: 何時(なんじ)に寝(ね)ますか？

___

第五章
だいごしょう
LESSON 5

TE-FORM OF VERBS IN JAPANESE

もくひょう **目標**	**OBJECTIVE**

✓ Learn how to change verbs into the te-forms.
✓ Learn how to form sentences using the te-form.

ないよう **内容**	**CONTENTS**

Section 1: Grammar

Section 1-1: How to Form the te-form

Section 1-2: Various Ways of Using the te-form

Section 1-3: Using the te-form to Describe More Than One Activity

Section 1-4: How to Explain What You Have Done Already

Section 2: Vocabulary

Section 3: Exercises

SECTION 1: GRAMMAR

SECTION 1-1: HOW TO FORM *TE*-FORM

Te-form is a conjugation pattern for verbs in Japanese. All the *te*-form verbs end with the hiragana character て (te) or で (de). The *te*-form is very useful and has many functions; for example, making a request, asking for permission, making "-ing" forms of verbs, and more. You learned the *te*-form of adjectives in lesson 3. In this section, you will learn how to form *te*-form of verbs.

- *ru*-verbs

To create a *te*-form, replace the final る with て.

Dictionary form	*te*-form
たべる	たべて

- *u*-verbs

The Conjugation patterns of *u*-verbs are a bit more complicated. In many instances, *u*-verbs can end in く *ku*, ぐ *gu*, す *su*, む *mu*, る *ru*, and more. Therefore, look at the final syllable of the dictionary form to know how to conjugate *u*-verbs.

1. *u*-verbs that end in く *ku*: Drop く and add いて

    かく → かいて

2. *u*-verbs that end in ぐ *gu*: Drop ぐ and add いで

    およぐ → およいで

3. *u*-verbs that end in す *su*: Drop す and add して

    はなす → はなして

4. *u*-verbs that end in む *mu*, ぶ *bu*, ぬ *nu*: Drop む, ぶ, ぬ and add んで

    のむ → のんで

5. *u*-verbs that end in う *u*, つ *tsu*, る *ru*: Drop う, つ, る and add って

つく<u>る</u>　→　つく<u>って</u>

The verb いく *iku* (to go) is a special exception and it doesn't follow the pattern above.

い<u>く</u>　→　<u>いって</u>

SECTION 1-2: VARIOUS WAYS OF USING THE *TE*-FORM

Now, let's see how to use *te*-forms.

I. *Te*-form + ください: Please do...

The *te*-form together with ください is used to make a polite request. When talking to a close friend or a family member, the *te*-form can be used as a request.

Examples:

<ruby>窓<rt>まど</rt></ruby>を<ruby>開<rt>あ</rt></ruby>けてください。　　Please open the window.

ちょっと<ruby>待<rt>ま</rt></ruby>って！　　Wait a minute!

II. *Te*-form + もいいです: You can do...

The *te*-form together with もいいです is used to describe an activity that is permitted. Often the hiragana character よ is added at the end of the sentences to soften the tone of voice. To ask for permission, the *te*-form is combined with もいいですか.

Examples:

<ruby>私<rt>わたし</rt></ruby>のペンを<ruby>使<rt>つか</rt></ruby>ってもいいですよ。　　You may use my pen.

<ruby>窓<rt>まど</rt></ruby>を<ruby>開<rt>あ</rt></ruby>けてもいいですか？　　May I open the window?

ええ、いいですよ。　　Yes, you may.

III. *Te*-form + はいけません: You cannot do...

To make a strong prohibition sentence, the *te*-form is combined with はいけません.

写真(しゃしん)を撮(と)ってはいけません。　　You must not take a picture.

お酒(さけ)を飲(の)んではいけません。　　You must not drink alcohol.

IV. *Te*-form + います

The *te*-form together with います has various functions. There are mainly three functions:

    1. An action in progress (-ing)

    2. Habit or occupation

    3. Current state or condition

- **An action in progress (〜ing)**

The *te*-form together with います is used to describe an action that you are doing now. It is similar to "ing" in English. See the examples below.

本(ほん)を読(よ)みます。　　I'm going to read a book. (Present tense)

本(ほん)を読(よ)んでいます。　　I'm reading a book. (*te*-form)

車(くるま)を運転(うんてん)します。　　I drive a car. (Present tense)

車(くるま)を運転(うんてん)しています。　　I'm driving a car. (*te*-form)

京都(きょうと)に住(す)みます。　　I'm going to live in Kyoto. (Present tense)

京都(きょうと)に住(す)んでいます。　　I live in Kyoto. (*te*-form)

- **Habit or occupation**

The *te*-form together with います is also used to describe what a person does for an occupation or a habit.

<ruby>毎日<rt>まいにち</rt></ruby>、<ruby>日本語<rt>にほんご</rt></ruby>を<ruby>勉強<rt>べんきょう</rt></ruby>しています。　　I study Japanese every day.

<ruby>大学<rt>だいがく</rt></ruby>で<ruby>経済学<rt>けいざいがく</rt></ruby>を<ruby>勉強<rt>べんきょう</rt></ruby>しています。　　I study economics at university.

<ruby>銀行<rt>ぎんこう</rt></ruby>で<ruby>働<rt>はたら</rt></ruby>いています。　　I work for a bank.

- **Current state or condition**

The *te*-form together with います is used to describe a current state, condition and appearance of something. See each sentence below.

<ruby>結婚<rt>けっこん</rt></ruby>します。　　I'm going to get married. (Present tense)

<ruby>結婚<rt>けっこん</rt></ruby>しました。　　I've gotten married. (Present perfect tense)

<ruby>結婚<rt>けっこん</rt></ruby>しています。　　I'm married. (*te*-form)

ジャケットを<ruby>着<rt>き</rt></ruby>ます。　　I'm going to wear a jacket. (Present tense)

ジャケットを<ruby>着<rt>き</rt></ruby>ました。　　I wore a jacket. (Past tense)

ジャケットを<ruby>着<rt>き</rt></ruby>ています。　　I'm wearing a jacket. (*te*-form)

<ruby>知<rt>し</rt></ruby>ります。　　I will know… (Present tense)

<ruby>知<rt>し</rt></ruby>りました。　　I got to know… (Past tense)

<ruby>知<rt>し</rt></ruby>っています。　　I know… (*te*-form)

SECTION 1-3: USING *TE*-FORM
TO DESCRIBE MORE THAN ONE ACTIVITY

In English, "and" can be used to describe more than one activity; for example, "I'm going to drink coffee and do my homework." In Japanese, *te*-form is used to combine two actions in one sentence to form a compound sentence. See the examples below.

コーヒーを飲みます。   I'm going to drink coffee.

宿題をします。   I'm going to do my homework.

コーヒーを<u>飲んで</u>、宿題をします。   I'm going to drink coffee and (then) do my homework.

One of the most common mistakes is using the particle と to combine two actions. But note that the particle と is used to connect two nouns but not verbs.

×コーヒーを飲<u>むと</u>、宿題をします。 (incorrect)

Since there is no past tense of *te*-form, a verb at the end of sentence defines the tense of the sentence.

5時に起きて、<u>勉強しました</u>。   I got up at 5 and studied.

朝ごはんを食べて、学校に<u>行きました</u>。   I ate breakfast and went to school.

SECTION 1-4: HOW TO EXPLAIN WHAT YOU HAVE DONE ALREADY

Adverbs もう and まだ are used to explain what you have done already or what you have not yet finished doing. もう is equivalent of "already" in English. On the other hand, まだ means "not yet" or "still", and this adverb is used with the negative form of verbs.

See the example sentences below.

もう宿題をしましたか？　　　　Have you already done your homework?

いえ、まだしていません。　　　No, I haven't done the homework yet.

もう朝ごはんを食べましたか？　　Have you eaten breakfast already?

いえ、まだ食べていません。　　　No, I haven't eaten breakfast yet.

ジョンはもうパーティ会場に着きましたか？　Has John arrived at the party venue already?

いえ、まだ着いていません。　　　No, he hasn't arrived yet.

Summary

もう + past tense: already done something

まだ + te-form: have not yet done something

SECTION 2: VOCABULARY

Ru-verbs

はじ
始める　to begin

あ
シャワーを浴びる　to take a shower

き
決める　to decide

おぼ
覚える　to remember, memorize

す
捨てる　to throw away

U-verbs

ある
歩く　to walk

てつだ
手伝う　to help, assist

つか
使う　to use

すわ
座る　to sit

はたら
働く　to work

さが
探す　to look for

まな
学ぶ　to learn

し
死ぬ　to die

す
住む　to live

あ
会う　to meet, see

はら
払う　to pay

あら
洗う　to wash

い
言う　to say

し
知る　to know

うた
歌う　to sing

と
撮る　to take (pictures), film

と
泊まる　to stay (hotel, accommodation)

Irregular verbs

けっこん
結婚する　to get married

れんしゅう
練習する　to practice

うんてん
運転する　to drive

でんわ
電話する　to call

りょうり
料理する　to cook

Study

しゅくだい
宿題　homework

きょうかしょ
教科書　textbook

けいざいがく
経済学　economics

ほうりつ
法律　law

れきし
歴史　history

けんちく
建築　architecture

SECTION 3: EXERCISES

SECTION 3-1: VOCABULARY

Practice 1: 単語を覚えよう
<small>たんご　おぼ</small>

Match the vocabulary that corresponds to the pictures.

① <small>す</small> 捨てる　•　　　　　　　　　　•　

② <small>てつだ</small> 手伝う　•　　　　　　　　　　•　

③ <small>あ</small> 会う　•　　　　　　　　　　　•　

④ <small>うた</small> 歌う　•　　　　　　　　　　　•　

⑤ <small>さが</small> 探す　•　　　　　　　　　　　•　

⑥ シャワーを浴<small>あ</small>びる　•　　　　　　　•　

⑦ <small>けっこん</small> 結婚する　•　　　　　　　　　•　

⑧ <small>うんてん</small> 運転する　•　　　　　　　　　•　

SECTION 3-2: READING AND WRITING

Practice 1: 動詞(どうし)

Below is a table of conjugation of the *te*-form. Carefully review it and complete the blank spaces.

	te-form		*te*-form
きる　to wear	きて	はなす	
おきる		きく	
でかける		てつだう	
みる		あそぶ	
おしえる		よむ	
あける		とまる	
しめる		うんてんする	

Practice 2: 文(ぶん)を書(か)こう

Translate the following sentences into Japanese.

Example: Please open the door.　ドアをあけてください。

① Please close the window. ＿＿＿＿＿＿＿＿＿＿＿＿＿＿＿＿＿＿。

② Please teach me Japanese. ＿＿＿＿＿＿＿＿＿＿＿＿＿＿＿＿＿。

③ Please listen to me. ＿＿＿＿＿＿＿＿＿＿＿＿＿＿＿＿＿＿＿。

④ Please read this textbook. ＿＿＿＿＿＿＿＿＿＿＿＿＿＿＿＿＿。

⑤ Please speak slowly. ＿＿＿＿＿＿＿＿＿＿＿＿＿＿＿＿＿＿。

⑥ Please practice playing the piano. ＿＿＿＿＿＿＿＿＿＿＿＿＿＿。

⑦ Please throw away the garbage. ＿＿＿＿＿＿＿＿＿＿＿＿＿＿＿。

⑧ Please call me tomorrow. ＿＿＿＿＿＿＿＿＿＿＿＿＿＿＿＿＿。

⑨ Please help me. _____。

⑩ Please watch this video. _____。

Practice 3: 質問(しつもん)しよう

Make sentences using てもいいですか to ask for permission to do the following things.

① to sit on a chair

_____

② to take pictures

_____

③ to use your friend's pen

_____

④ to speak English

_____

⑤ to play the guitar

_____

⑥ to close the window

_____

⑦ to go to the bathroom

_____

⑧ to open the door

_____

⑨ to throw away the garbage

_____

⑩ to drink a glass of wine

_____

Practice 4: 禁止（きんし）サイン

Match the signs and sentences below.

A. 入（はい）ってはいけません。

B. ここで食（た）べてはいけません。

C. 写真（しゃしん）を撮（と）ってはいけません。

D. 携帯電話（けいたいでんわ）を使（つか）ってはいけません。

E. ここで遊（あそ）んではいけません。

Practice 5: 何(なに)をしていますか

The table below shows what each student is doing. Describe the picture using the vocabulary under the image.

①ノア	②スカイ	③フアン	④ディアナ
にほんりょうり 日本料理	テニス	くるま 車	よる 夜ごはん
⑤サンディ	⑥トシ	⑦ソア	⑧ジョン
にほんご 日本語	カラオケ	ギター	ゲーム

① ノア
_____

② スカイ
_____

③ フアン
_____

④ ディアナ
_____

⑤ サンディ
_____

⑥ トシ
_____

⑦ ソア
_____

⑧ ジョン
_____

Practice 6: 自分(じぶん)のこと

Noa and Diana are talking about themselves. Read the passages below and answer the questions.

わたしはノアです。カナダのバンクーバーに住(す)んでいます。バンクーバーは大きくて、きれいな街(まち)です。わたしは大学(だいがく)で経済(けいざい)を勉強(べんきょう)しています。来年(らいねん)卒業(そつぎょう)します。もう仕事(しごと)は決(き)まりました。日本人(にほんじん)のガールフレンドがいます。でもまだ結婚(けっこん)していません。

Question 1: ノアはどこに住(す)んでいますか？

_____

Question 2: ノアは何(なに)を勉強(べんきょう)していますか？

_____

Question 3: ノアは結婚(けっこん)していますか？

_____

わたしはディアナです。アメリカのシカゴに住(す)んでいます。わたしは大学(だいがく)で医学(いがく)を勉強(べんきょう)しました。今(いま)は病院(びょういん)で働(はたら)いています。毎日(まいにち)とてもいそがしいです。土曜日(どようび)はいつもジムで運動(うんどう)しています。日曜日(にちようび)は家(いえ)で日本語(にほんご)を勉強(べんきょう)しています。

Question 4: ディアナはどこに住(す)んでいますか？

_____

Question 5: どこで働(はたら)いていますか？

_____

Question 6: 週末(しゅうまつ)は何(なに)をしていますか？

_____

Practice 7: 文（ぶん）をつなげよう

Combine two sentences using the *te*-form.

Example: 5時（じ）に起（お）きます。　ジョギングします。

5時（じ）に起（お）きて、ジョギングします。

① 6時（じ）に起（お）きます。　朝（あさ）ごはんを食（た）べます。

_____

② 新（あたら）しいドレスを着（き）ます。　パーティに行（い）きます。

_____

③ 電車（でんしゃ）にのります。　東京（とうきょう）に行（い）きます。

_____

④ 朝（あさ）ごはんを食（た）べます。　コーヒーを飲（の）みます。

_____

⑤ ギターをひきます。　うた（うた）を歌（うた）います。

_____

⑥ 図書館（としょかん）に行（い）きます。　日本語（にほんご）を勉強（べんきょう）します。

_____

⑦ テレビを見（み）ます。　ねます。

_____

⑧ 朝（あさ）ごはんを作（つく）ります。　そうじします。

_____

Practice 8: 文を書こう

Translate the following sentences into Japanese using the te-form.

① I went to the park and read a book.
_____

② I cleaned my room and did my homework.
_____

③ I drank some beer and sang a song.
_____

④ I took a shower and went to a restaurant.
_____

⑤ I stayed at my friend's house and played video games.
_____

Practice 9: 空白をうめよう

Fill in the blank spaces with もう or まだ.

① 来年日本に行きます。_____飛行機のチケットを買いました。でも_____ホテルは予約していません。

② A：_____薬をのみましたか？

　　B：いいえ、_____のんでいません。でも_____体調はよくなりました。

③ A：_____このゲームを買いましたか？

　　B：はい、_____買いました。でも、_____していません。

Practice 10: 質問に答えよう

Read the questions below and answer them in Japanese.

① もう宿題をしましたか？

はい、_____

② もう漢字を１００個覚えましたか？

いいえ、_____

③ もう仕事が見つかりましたか？

いいえ、_____

④ もう新しい車を買いましたか？

はい、_____

⑤ もうお皿を洗いましたか？

いいえ、_____

⑥ もうお金を払いましたか？

いいえ、_____

⑦ もう家族に電話しましたか？

はい、_____

⑧ もう今日の新聞を読みましたか？

いいえ、_____

SECTION 3-3: LISTENING EXERCISES

 Practice 1: 自己紹介(じこしょうかい)

Sky is talking about herself. Listen to the audio recording and answer the questions that follow.

Question 1: どこに住(す)んでいますか？

_____

Question 2: 何(なに)が好(す)きですか？

_____

Question 3: もう漢字(かんじ)を覚(おぼ)えましたか？

_____

Practice 2: 家族の紹介(かぞく しょうかい)

Alex shows a picture of his family. Listen to the audio and indicate if the sentences are true or false.

① 父(ちち)と母(はは)はシドニーに住(す)んでいます。　　(True / False)

② 兄(あに)はまだ結婚(けっこん)していません。　　(True / False)

③ 姉(あね)は銀行(ぎんこう)で働(はたら)いています。　　(True / False)

④ アレックスには４人(にん)のきょうだいがいます。　　(True / False)

第六章
LESSON 6

SHORT FORM

もくひょう **目標**	**OBJECTIVE**

✓ Learn how to change verbs into short forms.
✓ Learn how to form sentences using short form.

ないよう **内容**	**CONTENTS**

Section 1: Grammar

Section 1-1: Present Tense Short Form

Section 1-2: Informal Speech

Section 1-3: Past Tense Short Form

Section 1-4: Various Usages of Short Form

Section 1-5: How to Explain Reasons

Section 2: Vocabulary

Section 3: Exercises

SECTION 1: GRAMMAR

SECTION 1-1: PRESENT TENSE SHORT FORM

Short form is a paradigm of conjugation. It is called the "short form" because it is relatively shorter than the form you learned in lesson 4, which is called the "long form." The short form is also called the "plain form" or an "informal form."

There are mainly two ways to use the short form.

   1. To make an informal phrase.

   2. To combine with other words in the middle of sentences.

First, see how to form the short forms of verbs below.

Dictionary form		Long form	Short form
ru-verb	たべる to eat	たべます tabemasu	たべる taberu
		たべません tabemasen	たべない tabenai
u-verb	いく to go	いきます ikimasu	いく iku
		いきません ikimasen	いかない ikanai

As you can see above, the short form is the same as dictionary form. To change the long form into the short form negative, ない (**nai**) is substituted for ません (**masen**). In the case of u-verbs, anai is substituted for imasen. This basic conjugation rule is summarized below.

> ### Summary
> - For the affirmative short form, the same as the dictionary form.
> - For the negative short form of ru-verbs, drop **masen** and add **nai**.
> - For the negative short form of u-verbs, drop **-imasen** and add **-anai**.

Irregular verbs don't follow the rule above. See the list below.

irregular verbs	する *to do*	します shimasu	する suru
		しません shimasen	しない shinai
	くる *to come*	きます kimasu	くる kuru
		きません kimasen	こない konai

Take note that the verb ある that was covered in lesson 2 is an exception. See the conjugation pattern below.

Exception	ある *there is/are...*	あります arimasu	ある aru
		ありません arimasen	ない nai

SECTION 1-2 INFORMAL SPEECH

In this section, you learn how to create informal speech. There are mainly three ways to change any sentence to the casual form.

1. **Use the short form.**

2. **Drop particles.**

3. **Add よ or ね at the end of sentences.**

Short form is often used when speaking with close friends or family members as a sign of intimacy. See the example sentences below.

(Formal) コーヒーを飲(の)みますか？
(Informal) コーヒー飲(の)む？

Note the difference between the two sentences above. Both sentences can be translated as "Do you drink coffee?" But for the second sentence, the short form is used instead of the long form and the particle を and the question marker か were dropped. See more examples.

(Formal) 時間(じかん)がありますか？　　Do you have the time?
(Informal) 時間(じかん)ある？

(Formal) 今日(きょう)は勉強(べんきょう)しません。　　I won't study today.
(Informal) 今日(きょう)は勉強(べんきょう)しない。

(Formal) ジョンはスペイン語(ご)を話(はな)せません。　　John doesn't speak Spanish.
(Informal) ジョンはスペイン語(ご)話(はな)せないよ。

(Formal) サンディは学生(がくせい)じゃないです。　　Sandy is not a student.
(Informal) サンディは学生(がくせい)じゃないよ。

(Formal) この公園(こうえん)は大(おお)きいです。　　This park is big.
(Informal) この公園(こうえん)は大(おお)きいね。

SECTION 1-3: PAST TENSE SHORT FORM

This section shows how to form the past tense short form. To better understand the conjugation pattern, it may be helpful to compare it with te-form of verbs.

	Present tense short form	*te*-form	Past tense short form
Affirmative	たべる	たべて	たべた
Negative	たべない		たべなかった
Affirmative	いく	いって	いった
Negative	いかない		いかなかった
Affirmative	くる	きて	きた
Negative	こない		こなかった
Affirmative	する	して	した
Negative	しない		しなかった

Here is the summary of conjugation rules to form the past-tense short form.

> **Summary**
> - For the past tense affirmative short form, replace て with た and で with だ
> - For the past tense negative short form, replace い with かった

Just as with the present tense short form, the past tense short form is often used for informal speech. See the example below.

Formal Conversation:

サンディはどこに行きましたか？   Where did Sandy go?

サンディは日本に行きました。   Sandy went to Japan.

Informal Conversation:

サンディはどこに行ったの？   Where did Sandy go?

日本に行ったよ。   Sandy went to Japan.

SECTION 1-4: VARIOUS USAGES OF SHORT FORM

In this section, you will learn the different methods of utilizing the short form. It is used to combine other words to form new phrases.

I. The negative short form + でください：Please don't...

The negative short form together with でください is used for saying "Please do not…." See the examples below.

公園でお酒を飲まないでください。   Please don't drink alcohol in the park.

携帯電話を使わないでください。   Please do not use your cellphone.

II. The short form + つもりです: I'm planning to

The Japanese word つもり **tsumori** is used to express an intention to do something. When the short form is attached to つもりです, it is used to describe what a person is planning to do. The negative short form plus つもりです means "I'm planning on not doing something."

ラーメンを食(た)べるつもりです。　　I'm planning to eat ramen.

明日(あした)のパーティには行(い)かないつもりです。　　I don't intend to go to the party tomorrow.

III. The short form + と思(おも)います: I think that...

おもいます means "I think" in Japanese. To express "I think that…," the short form together with とおもいます is used.

明日(あした)はテストがあると思(おも)います。　　I think we have a test tomorrow.

ジョンはスペイン語(ご)を話(はな)せないと思(おも)います。　　I think John doesn't speak Spanish.

ディアナは納豆(なっとう)を食(た)べると思(おも)います。　　I think Diana eats natto beans.

You can use とおもいます when the sentence doesn't contain any verbs such as "I think he is a student" or "I think she is beautiful." When a noun or a な-adjective precedes とおもいます, だ needs to be added before とおもいます. See the example sentences below.

サンディはきれいだと思(おも)います。　　I think Sandy is beautiful.

アレックスは学生(がくせい)だと思(おも)います。　　I think Alex is a student.

IV. The past tense short form + ことがあります: I have done it before.

This phrase is used to describe your experience.

納豆(なっとう)を食(た)べたことがあります。　　I have eaten natto before.

その映画(えいが)を見(み)たことがあります。　　I have seen that movie before.

Using this phrase, you can also ask someone if they have experience in doing something. If you want to express "you haven't done it before," ありません or ないです is used instead of あります. In a casual conversation, the particle が is often dropped. See the example below.

<ruby>日本<rt>にほん</rt></ruby>に<u><ruby>行<rt>い</rt></ruby>った</u>ことがありますか？　　Have you ever been to Japan?

　　　いえ、(<ruby>行<rt>い</rt></ruby>ったこと) <u>ないです</u>。　　No, I haven't.

<ruby>富士山<rt>ふじさん</rt></ruby>に<u><ruby>登<rt>のぼ</rt></ruby>った</u>ことがありますか？　　Have you ever hiked Mt. Fuji?

　　　いえ、<u>ありません</u>。　　No, I haven't.

V. The short form + ほうがいいです：It would be better to...

This phrase is useful when you want to give your friends a kind suggestion or advice. When the advice is in the affirmative, the verb is in the past-tense short form. When the advice is in the negative, the verb is in the present-tense short form.

ピアノを<u><ruby>練習<rt>れんしゅう</rt></ruby>した</u>ほうがいいですよ。　　You'd better practice playing the piano.

あのパーティには<u><ruby>行<rt>い</rt></ruby>かない</u>ほうがいいですよ。　　It is better not to go to the party.

Note that the particle よ is added at the end of both sentences to soften the tone of the advice.

SECTION 1-5: HOW TO EXPLAIN REASONS

In this section, you will learn how to explain reasons for certain actions. As you learned in lesson 4, から *kara* is used as a particle to express the starting point of something. However, から *kara* is also used to explain reasons and it is somewhat similar to "because" in English.

Follow the sentence pattern below to explain reasons for actions.

> ### (reason) から、(situation)
> (situation) because (reason)

Examples:

<ruby>明日<rt>あした</rt></ruby>テストがある<u>から</u>、<ruby>勉強<rt>べんきょう</rt></ruby>します。　　I'm going to study because I have a test tomorrow.

<ruby>暑<rt>あつ</rt></ruby>い<u>から</u>、エアコンをつけます。　　I'm going to turn on the AC because it's hot.

ひま<u>だから</u>、テレビを<ruby>見<rt>み</rt></ruby>ます。　　I'm going to watch TV because I'm free.

<ruby>車<rt>くるま</rt></ruby>を<ruby>買<rt>か</rt></ruby>った<u>から</u>、お<ruby>金<rt>かね</rt></ruby>がありません。　　I have no money left because I bought a car.

Usually, the short form is used before から *kara*. When a noun or a な-adjective is used in a reason section, だから is used instead of から.

Summary

- Short form of verbs + から
- い -adjective + から
- な -adjective + <u>だ</u>から
- Noun + <u>だ</u>から

SECTION 2: VOCABULARY

Ru-verbs
<ruby>入<rt>い</rt></ruby>れる　to put in, to let in, to install
<ruby>壊<rt>こわ</rt></ruby>れる　to break, be broken
<ruby>疲<rt>つか</rt></ruby>れる　to get tired

U-verbs
<ruby>吸<rt>す</rt></ruby>う　to smoke, to suck
<ruby>履<rt>は</rt></ruby>く　to wear (shoes, pants)
なくす　to lose
<ruby>売<rt>う</rt></ruby>る　to sell

Irregular verbs
<ruby>入院<rt>にゅういん</rt></ruby>する　to be admitted into a hospital
<ruby>散歩<rt>さんぽ</rt></ruby>する　to take a walk

Adjective
<ruby>痛<rt>いた</rt></ruby>い　painful, to become hurt

Time
<ruby>今日<rt>きょう</rt></ruby>　today
<ruby>昨日<rt>きのう</rt></ruby>　yesterday
<ruby>明日<rt>あした</rt></ruby>　tomorrow
<ruby>明後日<rt>あさって</rt></ruby>　day after tomorrow
<ruby>週末<rt>しゅうまつ</rt></ruby>　weekend
<ruby>来週<rt>らいしゅう</rt></ruby>　next week
<ruby>先週<rt>せんしゅう</rt></ruby>　last week
<ruby>今週<rt>こんしゅう</rt></ruby>　this week

Seasons
<ruby>春<rt>はる</rt></ruby>　spring
<ruby>夏<rt>なつ</rt></ruby>　summer
<ruby>秋<rt>あき</rt></ruby>　fall / autumn
<ruby>冬<rt>ふゆ</rt></ruby>　winter

Other
<ruby>海外<rt>かいがい</rt></ruby>　abroad, overseas
パスポート　passport
<ruby>財布<rt>さいふ</rt></ruby>　wallet
<ruby>飛行機<rt>ひこうき</rt></ruby>　airplane
<ruby>結婚記念日<rt>けっこんきねんび</rt></ruby>　wedding anniversary
<ruby>買<rt>か</rt></ruby>い<ruby>物<rt>もの</rt></ruby>　shopping
<ruby>釣<rt>つ</rt></ruby>り　fishing
<ruby>歯医者<rt>はいしゃ</rt></ruby>　dentist
バー　bar
ケーキ　cake
<ruby>野菜<rt>やさい</rt></ruby>　vegetable
<ruby>日本料理<rt>にほんりょうり</rt></ruby>　Japanese cuisine

SECTION 3: EXERCISES

SECTION 3-1: VOCABULARY

Practice 1: 単語(たんご)を覚(おぼ)えよう

Match the vocabulary that corresponds to the pictures.

① 釣(つ)り • •

② 野菜(やさい) • •

③ 痛(いた)い • •

④ 飛行機(ひこうき) • •

⑤ 入院(にゅういん)する • •

⑥ 買(か)い物(もの) • •

⑦ 壊(こわ)れる • •

⑧ 財布(さいふ) • •

SECTION 3-2: READING AND WRITING

Practice 1: 動詞(どうし)

Below is a table of verbs. Change the long form verbs into the short form.

Dictionary form	Long form	Short form	Past tense short form
みる to see	みます		
	みません		
のむ to drink	のみます		
	のみません		
ねる to sleep	ねます		
	ねません		
よむ to read	よみます		
	よみません		
かく to write	かきます		
	かきません		
はなす to speak	はなします		
	はなしません		
あらう to wash	あらいます		
	あらいません		
やすむ to rest	やすみます		
	やすみません		
さがす to look for	さがします		
	さがしません		

Practice 2: 会話表現
かいわ ひょうげん

Read the questions below and change them into informal questions.

① どんな音楽を聞きますか？
　おんがく　き

_____

② よくバスにのりますか？

_____

③ 週末は何をしますか？
　しゅうまつ　なに

_____

④ もう朝ごはんは食べましたか？
　　あさ　　　　た

_____

⑤ もう宿題は終わりましたか？
　　しゅくだい　お

_____

Practice 3: 〜ないでください

Complete the sentences below to stop someone from doing something. Use the verbs provided in the box.

| いれる |
| あける |
| すう |
| とる |
| はしる |

① さむいから、窓を_____でください。
　　　　　　　まど

② ここで写真を_____でください。
　　　　しゃしん

③ あぶないから、_____でください。

④ コーヒーに砂糖を_____でください。
　　　　　　さとう

⑤ ここでタバコを_____でください。

Practice 4: 〜つもりです

Translate the following sentences using つもりです.

① I'm planning to buy a car.
_____

② I'm planning to go to the restaurant.
_____

③ I'm planning to study Spanish.
_____

④ I'm planning to go to bed at 9 o'clock.
_____

⑤ I'm planning to wear a jacket.
_____

⑥ I'm planning to look for a job in Japan.
_____

⑦ I'm planning to get married in fall.
_____

⑧ I don't intend to work on Sunday.
_____

⑨ I don't plan on going to the bar tonight.
_____

⑩ I'm not going to eat any cake.
_____

Practice 5: 何(なに)をするつもりですか

Look at the calendar below and answer the questions that follow.

曜日	すること
月曜日	仕事(しごと)
火曜日	仕事(しごと)
水曜日	仕事(しごと)
木曜日	昼:仕事(しごと) 夜(よる):ジム
金曜日	買(か)い物(もの)
土曜日	プール
日曜日	映画(えいが)

① 木曜日(もくようび)の夜(よる)は何(なに)をするつもりですか？

_____

② 金曜日(きんようび)は何(なに)をするつもりですか？

_____

③ 週末(しゅうまつ)は何(なに)をするつもりですか？

_____

④ 月曜日(げつようび)は何(なに)をするつもりですか？

_____

Practice 6: 〜とおもいます

Read the statements below and rewrite the sentences using と思います。

Example: ペコは肉を食べません。
→ ペコは肉を食べないと思います。

① サンディはプールで泳ぎます。
_____

② シンジはハイキングに行きます。
_____

③ アレックスは学生です。
_____

④ シカゴの冬は寒いです。
_____

⑤ エルサは日本語を話します。
_____

⑥ スカイはビールを飲みません。
_____

⑦ トシは学生じゃないです。
_____

⑧ フアンは新しい車を買いません。
_____

⑨ ディアナは日本のアニメを見ません。
_____

Practice 7: 〜したことがあります

Translate the following sentences into Japanese using ことがあります or ことがありません.

① I have been to Canada before.
_____

② I have made Japanese food before.
_____

③ I have listened to this song before.
_____

④ I have learned how to play the piano.
_____

⑤ I have had the experience of living abroad.
_____

⑥ I have never been to Kyoto.
_____

⑦ I have never written a letter to my parents.
_____

⑧ I have never swum in the sea.
_____

⑨ I have never read that book before.
_____

⑩ I have never watched that movie.
_____

Practice 8: 〜したことがありますか

Some personal questions have been prepared. Answer the questions below in Japanese.

① 富士山に登ったことがありますか？

_____

② ニューヨークに行ったことがありますか？

_____

③ ラーメンを食べたことがありますか？

_____

④ ビールを飲んだことがありますか？

_____

⑤ 新幹線に乗ったことがありますか？

_____

⑥ ドラえもんを見たことがありますか？

_____

⑦ 入院したことがありますか？

_____

⑧ 車を運転したことがありますか？

_____

⑨ テニスをしたことがありますか？

_____

⑩ 釣りをしたことがありますか？

_____

Practice 9: 〜ほうがいいですよ

Look at the picture below and choose the appropriate suggestion for them from A to D.

①
A．勉強した ほうがいいですよ。
B．朝ごはんを食べた ほうがいいですよ。
C．運動した ほうがいいですよ。
D．マスクをつけた ほうがいいですよ。

②
A．休んだ ほうがいいですよ。
B．働いた ほうがいいですよ。
C．走った ほうがいいですよ。
D．ビールを飲んだ ほうがいいですよ。

③
A．コーヒーを飲んだ ほうがいいですよ。
B．食べた ほうがいいですよ。
C．シャワーを浴びた ほうがいいですよ。
D．運動した ほうがいいですよ。

④
A．水を飲んだ ほうがいいですよ。
B．はやく寝た ほうがいいですよ。
C．ゲームした ほうがいいですよ。
D．テレビを見た ほうがいいですよ。

⑤
A．散歩に行った ほうがいいですよ。
B．仕事を探した ほうがいいですよ。
C．食べた ほうがいいですよ。
D．日本語を練習した ほうがいいですよ。

⑥

A．そうじしたほうがいいですよ。
B．勉強したほうがいいですよ。
C．野菜を食べたほうがいいですよ。
D．お酒を飲まないほうがいいですよ。

Practice 10: アドバイスしよう

Below is a combination of situations and challenges faced by regular people. Give advice using ほうがいいですよ.

Example: 歯が痛いです。　　I have a toothache.

Advice: 歯医者に行ったほうがいいですよ。　　You'd better go to the dentist.

① 頭が痛いです。

_____

② 今日はとても暑いです。

_____

③ パスポートをなくしました。

_____

④ 明日は両親の結婚記念日です。

_____

⑤ 明日テストがあります。

_____

⑥ 友だちが家に来ます。

_____

⑦ パソコンが壊れました。

_____

⑧ 宿題がむずかしいです。

_____

Practice 11: 〜から

Below are scenarios of people choosing to do or not do something. Select the most appropriate reason (A–D) that explains their decision.

① (　　　　　　　)から、運動しません。

A. おいしい　　　B. すずしい　　　C. たかい　　　D. びょうきだ

② (　　　　　　　)から、日本語を勉強します。

A. テレビをみる　　B. 日本にいく　　C. ねむい　　　D. やすい

③ (　　　　　　　)から、買いません。

A. おいしい　　　B. すずしい　　　C. たかい　　　D. テストがある

④ (　　　　　　　)から、窓を開けてください。

A. さむい　　　　B. あつい　　　　C. たかい　　　D. あたらしい

⑤ (　　　　　　　)から、お金がありません。

A. そうじした　　B. くるまをかった　C. うんどうした　D. ねむい

Practice 12: 文（ぶん）を作（つく）ろう

Match the statement given with an appropriate reason.

① 音楽（おんがく）が好（す）きだから　●　　　●　プールで泳（およ）ぎます。

② 飛行機（ひこうき）は高（たか）いから　●　　　●　部屋（へや）をそうじします。

③ 兄（あに）が結婚（けっこん）するから　●　　　●　バスを使（つか）います。

④ 今日（きょう）はあついから　●　　　●　ピアノを習（なら）います。

⑤ 友（とも）だちが家（いえ）に来（く）るから　●　　　●　プレゼントを買（か）います。

Practice 13: 文（ぶん）を書（か）こう

Translate following sentences into Japanese using から.

① I'm not sleepy because I drank coffee.

_____

② I'm not going out because I have a test tomorrow.

_____

③ I'm going to buy a new computer because my computer is broken.

_____

④ I bought medication because my mother is sick.

_____

⑤ I'm going home because I'm tired.

_____

Practice 14: あなたの意見(いけん)

Look at the picture of Juan and formulate your opinion about him using とおもいます to answer each question.

① 背(せ)が高(たか)いですか？

_____

② やさしいですか？

_____

③ 日本語(にほんご)を話(はな)しますか？

_____

④ ギターをひきますか？

_____

SECTION 3-3: LISTENING EXERCISES

 Practice 1: 会話を聴き取ろう
かいわ　き　と

Sandy and Noa are chatting about her trip. Listen to their conversation and answer the questions that follow.

Question 1: ノアは京都に行ったことがありますか？
きょうと　い

_____

Question 2: ノアは新幹線に乗ったことがありますか？
しんかんせん　の

_____

Question 3: サンディは大阪に行ったことがありますか？
おおさか　い

_____

 Practice 2: アドバイスを聞こう
き

Alex and Toshi are talking. Listen to their conversation and write down Toshi's suggestions to improve his Japanese.

① _____

② _____

Japanese Grammar Made Easy | Lesson 6 | Section 3   141

第七章
だいななしょう
LESSON 7

DESCRIBE WHAT YOU WANT TO DO

<ruby>目標<rt>もくひょう</rt></ruby>	**OBJECTIVE**

✓ Learn how to describe what you want to do and what other people want to do.

<ruby>内容<rt>ないよう</rt></ruby>	**CONTENTS**

Section 1: Grammar

Section 1-1: Describe What You Want to Do

Section 1-2: Describe What Someone Else Wants to Do

Section 1-3: Things You Want

Section 1-4: Using "When…"

Section 1-5: Describe the Purpose of Movement

Section 2: Vocabulary

Section 3: Exercises

SECTION 1: GRAMMAR

SECTION 1-1: DESCRIBE WHAT YOU WANT TO DO

"I want to go to the bathroom," "I want to drink some coffee," "I want to study Japanese." Describing your needs and desires is an important part of conversation. In this lesson, you will learn how to describe your hopes or aspirations.

The *tai*-form is used to express the desire to do something. Creating a *tai*-form sentence is fairly simple. All you need to do is to add たい after the verb stem. The auxiliary verb です (***desu***) can be added to sound more polite. See the conjugation rules and the table of examples below.

Conjugation Rule to Create a *Tai*-form

Verb stem + たい

I want to...

Short form	Long form	*tai*-form
たべる to eat	たべます	たべたい I want to eat...
のむ to drink	のみます	のみたい I want to drink...
かう to buy	かいます	かいたい I want to buy...
はなす to speak	はなします	はなしたい I want to speak...
する to do	します	したい I want to do...

トイレに行きたいです。　　I want to go to the bathroom.

コーヒーが飲みたいです。　　I want to drink some coffee.

日本語を勉強したいです。　　I want to study Japanese.

The box below illustrates how to compose the negative, past, past negative form of the *tai*-form.

Negative: verb stem + たくない
I don't want to...

Negative form examples:

コーヒーは飲みたくないです。　　I don't want to drink coffee.

学校に行きたくないです。　　I don't want to go to school.

Past: verb stem + たかった
I wanted to...

Past form examples:

コーヒーが飲みたかったです。　　I wanted to drink some coffee.

日本に行きたかったです。　　I wanted to go to Japan.

Past negative: verb stem + たくなかった
I didn't want to...

Past negative form examples:

肉は食べたくなかったです。　　I didn't want to eat meat.

宿題をしたくなかったです。　　I didn't want to do my homework.

SECTION 1-2: DESCRIBE WHAT SOMEONE ELSE WANTS TO DO

Usually, the *tai*-form is used to describe a personal desire, but not someone else's desire. Since we can't read another person's mind and the inner thoughts and feelings are known only by the person feeling them, in Japanese, someone else's desires are usually reported as quotations or observations. There are a couple of ways to express someone else's desires.

> **〜たがっています**
>
> *It seems like they want to...*

When you observe that someone seemingly wants to do something, you can use this form. You simply need to use たがっています instead of たい. See the examples below.

Examples:

サンディはスイカを<u>食べたがっています</u>。　It seems like Sandy wants to eat a piece of a watermelon.

シンジは温泉に<u>入りたがっています</u>。　It seems like Shinji wants to go to the onsen.

> **Tai-form + と言っていました**
>
> *They said that they want to...*

To quote someone saying that they want to do something, you can use といっていました with *tai*-form.

Examples:

サンディはスイカを食べたい<u>と言っていました</u>。　Sandy said that she wants to eat a piece of a watermelon.

シンジは温泉に入りたい<u>と言っていました</u>。　Shinji said that he wants to go to the onsen.

> ## *Tai*-form + そうです / らしいです
> ### I heard that they want to...

そうです means "I heard that." This phrase can be used together with the tai-form to express someone else's desire. そうです is rather formal and らしいです is more conversational.

Examples:

サンディはスイカを食べたい<u>そうです</u>。　　I heard that Sandy wants to eat a piece of a watermelon.

シンジは温泉に入りたい<u>らしいです</u>。　　I heard that Shinji wants to go to the onsen.

> ## *Tai*-form + って
> ### I heard that they want to...

Just as the phrase そうです, って also means "I heard that." However, it is used together with *tai*-form only in casual settings.

Examples:

サンディはスイカ食べたい<u>って</u>。　　I heard that Sandy wants to eat a piece of a watermelon.

シンジは温泉に入りたい<u>って</u>。　　I heard that Shinji wants to go to the onsen.

SECTION 1-3: THINGS YOU WANT

The word ほしい *(hoshii)* is an い-adjective that is used to express the things you want. While the *tai*-form is used to describe the action you want to take, ほしい is used with nouns. See the basic structure below.

〜がほしい
I want (something)

Note that the object is usually followed by the particle が.

Examples:

新しい車が <u>ほしい</u> です。　　I want a new car.

コーヒーが <u>ほしい</u> です。　　I want a cup of coffee.

Because the word ほしい is an い- adjective, the conjugation patterns to form the negative, past and past negative are the same as other い- adjectives.

新しい車は <u>ほしくない</u> です。　　I don't want a new car. (negative)

新しい車が <u>ほしかった</u> です。　　I wanted a new car. (past)

新しい車は <u>ほしくなかった</u> です。　　I didn't want a new car. (past negative)

Note that the particle は is often used in a negative sentence.

Just as with the tai-form, ほしい is exclusively used for the first person, the speaker. When describing someone else's desire, the quotations or observations form should be used.

ジョンは新しい車がほしいと <u>言っていました</u>。　　John said that he wants a new car.

ジョンは新しい車がほしい <u>そうです</u>。　　I heard that John wants a new car.

ジョンは新しい車がほしい <u>って</u>。　　I heard that John wants a new car. (casual)

SECTION 1-4: USING "WHEN…"

時 (とき) is used to describe "when" something happened. とき can be used together with a noun, a verb, and an adjective. See the basic structure below.

> **Short form of verbs + とき**
>
> **い- adjective + とき**
>
> **な- adjective + とき**
>
> **Noun + のとき**

Note that the particle の must be added when a noun precedes とき.

Examples:

日本に行った時、温泉に入りました。　　When I went to Japan, I went to a hot spring

暑い時はエアコンをつけてください。　　When it's hot, use the air conditioner.

暇な時、電話してください。　　When you have some time, please call me.

子どもの時、英語を勉強しました。　　When I was a child, I studied English.

SECTION 1-5: DESCRIBING THE PURPOSE OF MOVEMENT

If you want to explain the purpose of movement, such as "I'm going to the library to read books" or "I'm going to my friend's house to watch the World Cup," follow the sentence structure below.

> **Verb stem + に行く**
>
> *I go to… in order to do something*

Examples:

<ruby>図書館<rt>としょかん</rt></ruby>へ <u><ruby>本<rt>ほん</rt></ruby>を<ruby>読<rt>よ</rt></ruby>み</u>に<ruby>行<rt>い</rt></ruby>きます。　　I'm going to the library <u>to read books</u>.

<ruby>友<rt>とも</rt></ruby>だちの<ruby>家<rt>いえ</rt></ruby>に<u>ワールドカップを<ruby>見<rt>み</rt></ruby></u>に<ruby>行<rt>い</rt></ruby>きました。

I went to my friend's house <u>to watch the World Cup</u>.

In the example sentences above, the underlined portion shows the purpose. You can place the location (the goal of movement) either before or after that purpose phrase.

<ruby>日本語<rt>にほんご</rt></ruby>を<ruby>勉強<rt>べんきょう</rt></ruby>しに<u><ruby>日本<rt>にほん</rt></ruby></u>に<ruby>行<rt>い</rt></ruby>きます。　　I'm going to Japan to study Japanese.

<u><ruby>日本<rt>にほん</rt></ruby></u>に<ruby>日本語<rt>にほんご</rt></ruby>を<ruby>勉強<rt>べんきょう</rt></ruby>しに<ruby>行<rt>い</rt></ruby>きます。　　I'm going to Japan to study Japanese.

SECTION 2: VOCABULARY

Verbs
りゅうがく
留学する   to study abroad

Occupations
せんしゅ
選手   (sports) player
かいしゃ
会社   company
けいさつ
警察   police
ほんやく
翻訳   translation
かしゅ
歌手   singer
ぎんこういん
銀行員   banker
がくしゃ
学者   scholar

Foods
アイスクリーム   ice cream
にほんしゅ
日本酒   Japanese sake
くだもの
果物   fruit
さとう
砂糖   sugar
しお
塩   salt
みず
水   water
にく
肉   meat
ぎゅうにゅう
牛乳   milk

Locations
やっきょく
薬局   pharmacy
びじゅつかん
美術館   art museum
おんせん
温泉   onsen (hot spring)

やま
山   mountain
かわ
川   river
いけ
池   pond
うみ
海   sea
みずうみ
湖   lake

Objects
くすり
薬   medicine
くつした
靴下   socks
めがね   eye glasses
てがみ
手紙   letter
タバコ   tobacco
ぬいぐるみ   stuffed toy
プレゼント   present
ペット   pet
うんてんめんきょ
運転免許   driver's license

Other
かねも
お金持ち   rich person
きゅうじつ
休日   holiday
しけん
試験   exam

SECTION 3: EXERCISES

SECTION 3-1: VOCABULARY

Practice 1: 単語を覚えよう
<small>たんご　おぼ</small>

Match the vocabulary that corresponds to the pictures.

① 薬局 <small>やっきょく</small>

② 温泉 <small>おんせん</small>

③ お金持ち <small>かねも</small>

④ 運転免許 <small>うんてんめんきょ</small>

⑤ 牛乳 <small>ぎゅうにゅう</small>

⑥ 日本酒 <small>にほんしゅ</small>

⑦ 警察 <small>けいさつ</small>

⑧ 翻訳 <small>ほんやく</small>

152　Section 3 | Lesson 7 | *Japanese Grammar Made Easy*

SECTION 3-2: READING AND WRITING

Practice 1: *tai*-form

A chart of the *tai*-form is provided below. Complete the conjugation table below.

Short form	*tai*-form	
	affirmative	negative
いく		
やすむ		
なる		
あう		
はたらく		
りゅうがくする		
ならう		
のる		

Practice 2: 〜たいです

Change the following statement sentences into "I want to" sentences using the tai-form.

Example: 海に行きます。 → 海に行きたいです。

① 日本語を勉強します。

___

② 彼女と結婚します。

___

③ 日本に留学します。

___

④ 車を買います。

___

Practice 3: ～たいですか

Read the questions below and answer using たいです for things you want to do or たくないです for things you don't want to do.

① 日本語を勉強したいですか？
_____

② 富士山に登りたいですか？
_____

③ 日本で働きたいですか？
_____

④ バンクーバーに行きたいですか？
_____

⑤ 歌手になりたいですか？
_____

⑥ 温泉に入りたいですか？
_____

⑦ すしを食べたいですか？
_____

⑧ 新幹線に乗りたいですか？
_____

⑨ 家を買いたいですか？
_____

Practice 4: 文章を作ろう

Rearrange the following sentences in the correct order.

① 家で / したいです / 休日は / ゆっくり

_____

② から / プールで / あつい / 泳ぎたいです

_____

③ カメラが / とるのが / すきだ / 写真を / から / 新しい / ほしいです

_____

④ から / 毎日 / ほしいです / 忙しい / 時間が

_____

⑤ つかれた / から / ねたいです / 家で

_____

Practice 5: 文をつなげよう

Match the statement sentences with the appropriate reason.

① 日本に行きたいから　　　•　　　•　車を運転したいです。

② 運転免許をとったから　　•　　　•　水を飲みたいです。

③ 試験が終わったから　　　•　　　•　日本語を勉強します。

④ お金がないから　　　　　•　　　•　買い物に行きたくないです。

⑤ あついから　　　　　　　•　　　•　友だちと遊びたいです。

Practice 6: 文章を書こう

Examine each picture carefully to infer what the people are thinking. Write one or more sentences using たいです or たくないです. Incorporate the vocabulary provided above each picture.

① しごと

④ おさけ

② コーヒー

⑤ シャワー

③ やさい

⑥ サッカーせんしゅ

Practice 7: したかったです

Translate the following sentences into Japanese.

① I wanted to learn to play the piano.
_____

② I wanted to fly in an airplane.
_____

③ I wanted to play video games.
_____

④ I wanted to have a pet.
_____

⑤ I wanted to go to California.
_____

⑥ I didn't want to watch that movie.
_____

⑦ I didn't want to drink coffee.
_____

⑧ I didn't want to meet him.
_____

⑨ I didn't want to study abroad.
_____

⑩ I didn't want to drive.
_____

⑪ I didn't want to go to the party.
_____

Practice 8: 何をしたかった？

Write five things you wanted to do and five things you didn't want to do when you were a child.

Example: 子どもの時、サッカー選手になりたかったです。　*I wanted to be a soccer player.*

What you wanted to do	What you didn't want to do
①	①
②	②
③	③
④	④
⑤	⑤

Practice 9: ほしいです

You want to receive the following items as gifts. Formulate sentences using ほしいです.

Practice 10: ほしくないです

You don't want the following items as gifts. Write sentences to explain that using ほしくないです.

Practice 11: 何(なに)がほしいですか

Read the following questions below and write your own answer.

Example: どんな時計(とけい)がほしいですか？

→ あたらしいスマートウォッチがほしいです。

① どんな日本(にほん)のおみやげがほしいですか？

_____

② どんな車(くるま)がほしいですか？

_____

③ どんな家(いえ)がほしいですか？

_____

④ 子どもの頃、何がほしかったですか？

_____

⑤ 今、何がいちばんほしいですか？

_____

Practice 12: みんながしたいこと

Report what the following people said, using といっています.

①  着物を着たいです。
サンディ

_____

②  ダンスパーティに行きたいです。
ディアナ

_____

③  お金持ちになりたいです。
ジョン

_____

④  ピアノを練習したくないです。
アレックス

_____

⑤  日本酒を飲みたいです。
トシ

_____

Practice 13: 何をしたいですか

Diana, John, Alex, and Sandy are expressing what they want. Read the passage below and answer the questions that follow.

---

① ディアナ

私の車は古くて小さいから、新しい車がほしいです。大きな日本車を買いたいです。シカゴからカリフォルニアまでドライブしたいです。カリフォルニアに友だちがいるから、友だちとディズニーランドで遊びたいです。

Question 1: ディアナはなにがほしいですか？

A. 小さい車　　B. 新しい車　　C. カメラ　　D. 友だち

Question 2: ディアナはカリフォルニアで何をしたいですか？

_____

---

② ジョン

日本中旅行したいです。まず、東京でスカイツリーに登りたいです。つぎに大阪に行って、たこ焼きを食べたいです。その後、京都に行って、古いお寺を見たいです。最後に沖縄に行って、海で泳ぎたいです。

Question 1: ジョンは何が食べたいですか？

A. たこ焼き　　B. 大阪　　C. お寺　　D. すし

Question 2: ジョンは京都で何をしたいですか？

_____

Question 3: ジョンは沖縄で何をしたいですか？

_____

③ アレックス

ぼくは学校で日本語を勉強しています。日本語がもっと上手になりたいです。だから日本人の友だちがほしいです。来年は日本に留学したいです。日本で勉強して、将来は日本で働きたいです。

Question 1: アレックスはどこで勉強したいですか？

A．学校　　　　B．アメリカ　　　　C．将来　　　　D．日本

Question 2: アレックスは来年何をしたいですか？

_____

④ サンディ

私と夫は動物が大好きだから、ペットがほしいです。夫は犬がほしいといっています。毎日犬と散歩したいそうです。私は子どもの頃、ねこを飼っていたから、ねこがほしいです。犬の散歩はしたくないです。

Question 1: サンディとサンディの夫は何がほしいですか？

A．子ども　　　　B．散歩　　　　C．ペット　　　　D．車

Question 2: サンディは何をしたくないですか？

_____

Practice 14: 〜に行きます。

Look at the chart below and make sentences like the example shown below.

Name	Where	Purpose
ソア	公園	散歩する
アレックス	友だちの家	テレビゲームをする
トシ	公園	桜を見る
フアン	郵便局	手紙を出す
スカイ	コンビニ	おにぎりを買う
ノア	スタバ	友だちに会う
ジョン	薬局	薬を買う

Example: ソアは公園に散歩しに行きました。

① アレックス
_____

② トシ
_____

③ フアン
_____

④ スカイ
_____

⑤ ノア
_____

⑥ ジョン
_____

SECTION 3-3: LISTENING EXERCISES

 Practice 1: 会話(かいわ)を聴(き)き取(と)ろう

Sky and Soa are making plans for the holiday. Listen to the recording and indicate if the sentences are true or false.

① ソアは働(はたら)きたい。 (True/False)

② スカイは新(あたら)しいジャケットがほしい。 (True/False)

③ ソアはカラオケに行(い)きたくない。 (True/False)

 Practice 2: 夏休(なつやす)みにしたいこと

Alex is talking about what he wants to do during his summer vacation. Please listen to the audio recording and answer the questions below.

Question 1: アレックスは何(なに)をしたくないですか？

_____

Question 2: アレックスのお父(とう)さんは何(なに)をしたいですか？

_____

Question 3: アレックスは漢字(かんじ)を何個(なんこ)おぼえたいですか？

_____

CONCLUSION

Congratulations on successfully finishing the very first step of learning Japanese grammar. Although there are certainly more things to learn in your language journey, this book has helped you to build a solid grammatical foundation. Imagine how much more accurate, varied, and meaningful your expressions have grown in Japanese just by simply completing this user friendly, interactive, and enjoyable basic grammar guide book. You can express what you did, what you are going to do, what you want and more! Everything that was covered in this book will definitely prove to be a great advantage as you put your knowledge to practice and to continue your language journey with us.

We encourage you to keep the numbered points below in mind to ensure your language learning efforts yield the best possible results.

1. Review this book

We have said it before and we will say it again: take care to review this book from time to time even after you finish all the practice sections. A solid grammatical foundation is the key to speaking a native-speaker-level Japanese and to perfectly understand when it is spoken to you. Use the vocabulary pages effectively by setting a goal to review and memorize a set number of words daily or weekly.

2. Use what you learned in this book

When it comes to learning a language, even polyglots admit that if we don't use it, we'll forget easily. This book provides sufficient grammatical knowledge to be able to write a diary, text message, and email friends and acquaintances in Japanese. Make it your daily habit to write short phrases, short sentences, and short messages in Japanese.

3. There are always exceptions

Please do not be shocked when native speakers don't follow the grammar rules you have learned in this book. There are always exceptions. If you ask them why they say something in a certain way, they will probably respond "Well, that's just the way it's said, but I do not know the reason behind it." When that happens, remember that the role of grammar is to explain language but that the speakers of that language can use it without strictly following those guidelines. Native speakers make the rules, not the grammar book. With that being said, be flexible and open to incorporate native expressions into your vocabulary.

It has been a pleasure to share this grammatical journey with you, and we warmly commend your efforts and dedication to learning Japanese. To support you further, we have prepared additional resources for learners like you to continue this lifelong pursuit.

Books like *"Lingo Mastery's Japanese Kanji Made Easy"* are excellent resources for students to develop their kanji writing skills. Wishing you all the best in your continued journey of learning Japanese!

ANSWER KEY

LESSON 1

SECTION 3-1: VOCABULARY

Practice 1

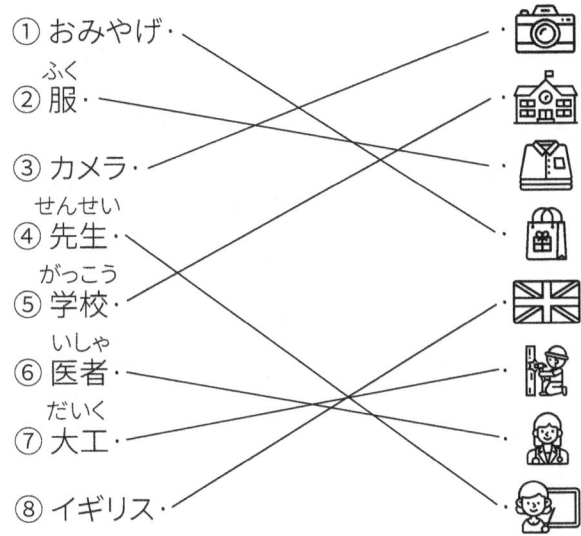

⑨ くるまのえ

⑩ がっこうのとしょかん

Practice 2

① わたしはがくせいです。

② おとうとはだいがくせいです。

③ あには20さいです。

④ ちちはかいしゃいんです。

⑤ ははしゅふです。

SECTION 3-2: READING AND WRITING

Practice 1

① わたしのいぬ

② わたしのカメラ

③ わたしのくるま

④ わたしのおとうさん

⑤ わたしのおとうと

⑥ サンディのいえ

⑦ カナダのがくせい

⑧ にほんのだいがく

Practice 3

① わたしのくるまです。
わたしのくるまじゃないです。

② わたしのおかあさんです。
わたしのおかあさんじゃないです。

③ わたしのおにいさんです。
わたしのおにいさんじゃないです。

④ わたしはイギリス人です。
わたしはイギリス人じゃないです。

⑤ わたしのがっこうです。
わたしのがっこうじゃないです。

Japanese Grammar Made Easy | Answer Key 167

⑥ わたしはだいがくせいです。

わたしはだいがくせいじゃないです。

⑦ わたしのおとうさんはエンジニアです。

わたしのおとうさんはエンジニアじゃないです。

⑧ わたしのおとうとは18さいです

わたしのおとうとは18さいじゃないです。

Practice 4

① ジョンさんですか？

② だいがくせいですか？

③ あなたのスマホですか？

④ 日本人ですか？

⑤ アメリカのしゃしんですか？

⑥ がっこうのせんせいでしたか？

⑦ サンディのくるまですか？

Practice 5

① いいえ、サンディはアメリカ人じゃないです。

② はい、ディアナはメキシコ人です。

③ いいえ、ジョンはかいしゃいんじゃないです。

④ はい、アレックスはがくせいです。

⑤ はい、トシはせんせいです。

Practice 6

サンディ　（B）

ディアナ　（D）

ジョン　　（C）

アレックス　（E）

トシ　　　（A）

Practice 8

① わたしはがくせいでした。

② おとうさんはがっこうのせんせいでした。

③ おかあさんはしゅふじゃなかったです。

④ おにいさんはかいしゃいんじゃなかったです。

⑤ おねえさんはだいがくせいでした。

SECTION 3-3: LISTENING EXERCISES

 Practice 1

はじめまして。私(わたし)はフアンです。メキシコ人です。学生(がくせい)です。17才(さい)です。

はじめまして。私(わたし)の名前(なまえ)はノアです。カナダ人(じん)です。大学生(だいがくせい)です。21才(さい)です。

はじめまして。私(わたし)はスカイです。アメリカ人(じん)です。英語(えいご)の先生(せんせい)です。25才(さい)です。

はじめまして。私(わたし)はソアです。韓国人(かんこくじん)です。私(わたし)はエンジニアです。27才(さい)です。

	Name	Nationality	Occupation/School	Age
①	フアン	メキシコ	がくせい	17
②	ノア	カナダ	だいがくせい	21
③	スカイ	アメリカ	えいごのせんせい	25
④	ソア	かんこく	エンジニア	27

Practice 2

これが私の家族です。お父さんはアメリカ人です。お母さんは韓国人です。お父さんの仕事は医者で、お母さんは主婦です。弟はまだ２０歳で、大学生です。

① False　　　② True　　　③ True

LESSON 2

SECTION 3-1: VOCABULARY

Practice 1

① かさ
② 時計 (とけい)
③ つくえ
④ 駐車場 (ちゅうしゃじょう)
⑤ 本 (ほん)
⑥ 冷蔵庫 (れいぞうこ)
⑦ リンゴ
⑧ 誕生日 (たんじょうび)

SECTION 3-2: READING AND WRITING

Practice 1

① B
② A
③ B
④ C

Practice 2

① <u>この</u>本はいくらですか？

② <u>あの</u>服はいくらですか？

③ <u>その</u>辞書はいくらですか？

④ <u>あの</u>時計はいくらですか？

⑤ <u>あの</u>靴はいくらですか？

Practice 3

① 弟が二人（います）

② 学校にさくらの木が（あります）

③ 私の家にテレビが（あります）

④ 冷蔵庫にリンゴが（あります）

⑤ 車の上にねこが（います）

Practice 4

① ねこがちゅうしゃじょうにいます。

② トイレにかみがありません。

③ アメリカ人のともだちがいます。

④ レストランにねずみがいます。

⑤ としょかんにほんがあります。

Practice 5

① 教室につくえがあります。

② 教室にせんせいがいます。

③ 教室にはながあります。

④ 教室にパソコンがありません。

⑤ 教室にエアコンがありません。

Practice 6

① ねこが3びきいます。

② ほんが4さつあります。

③ きっぷが2まいあります。

④ たまごが10こあります。

⑤ ワインが3ぼんあります。

⑥ がくせいが5にんいます。

⑦ かさが5ほんあります。

Practice 7

① つくえのしたにいぬがいます。

② おとこのひとがふたりいます。

③ まどのうえにとけいがあります。

④ つくえのうえにパソコンがあります。

SECTION 3-3: LISTENING EXERCISES

 Practice 1

これが僕の通っている日本語学校です。
日本語学校の左には図書館があります。
右には映画館があります。映画館のとなりには郵便局があります。私の家は公園のとなりです。

① A

② C

③ B

Practice 2

アレックス：すいません。日本語学校（にほんごがっこう）はここですか？

男の人：いいえ、ここは図書館（としょかん）ですよ。日本語学校（にほんごがっこう）は、あっちです。

アレックス：え？どこですか？

男の人：図書館（としょかん）の北（きた）に公園（こうえん）があります。公園（こうえん）のとなりに日本語学校（にほんごがっこう）がありますよ。

アレックス：わかりました。ありがとうございます。

① A

② としょかんのきたにこうえんがあります。

③ こうえんのとなりににほんごがっこうがあります。

LESSON 3

SECTION 3-1: VOCABULARY

 Practice 1

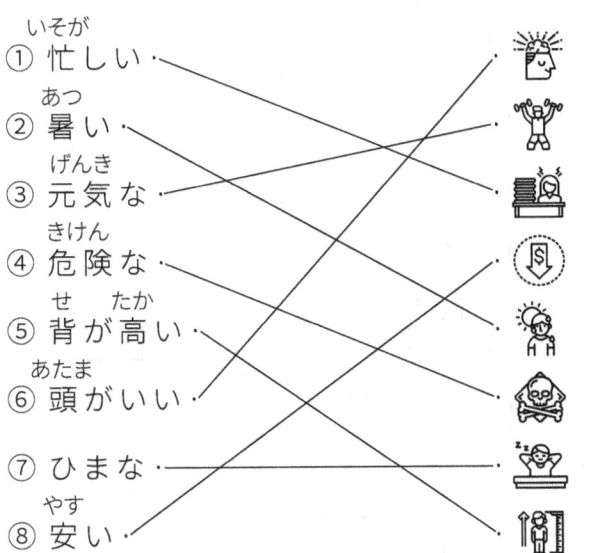

① 忙しい（いそが）
② 暑い（あつ）
③ 元気な（げんき）
④ 危険な（きけん）
⑤ 背が高い（せ たか）
⑥ 頭がいい（あたま）
⑦ ひまな
⑧ 安い（やす）

SECTION 3-2: READING AND WRITING

Practice 1

① い-adjectives

Plain form	Present		Past	
	Affirmative	Negative	Affirmative	Negative
おもしろい (interesting)	おもしろい	おもしろくない	おもしろかった	おもしろくなかった
ちいさい (small)	ちいさい	ちいさくない	ちいさかった	ちいさくなかった
ながい (long)	ながい	ながくない	ながかった	ながくなかった
みじかい (short)	みじかい	みじかくない	みじかかった	みじかくなかった
あつい (hot)	あつい	あつくない	あつかった	あつくなかった
さむい (cold)	さむい	さむくない	さむかった	さむくなかった
いそがしい (busy)	いそがしい	いそがしくない	いそがしかった	いそがしくなかった
ひろい (spacious)	ひろい	ひろくない	ひろかった	ひろくなかった
せまい (narrow)	せまい	せまくない	せまかった	せまくなかった
わるい (bad)	わるい	わるくない	わるかった	わるくなかった
やすい (cheap)	やすい	やすくない	やすかった	やすくなかった
たかい (expensive)	たかい	たかくない	たかかった	たかくなかった
おいしい (delicious)	おいしい	おいしくない	おいしかった	おいしくなかった
あたらしい (new)	あたらしい	あたらしくない	あたらしかった	あたらしくなかった
むずかしい (difficult)	むずかしい	むずかしくない	むずかしかった	むずかしくなかった

② な-adjectives

Plain form	Present		Past	
	Affirmative	Negative	Affirmative	Negative
げんきな (healthy)	げんき	げんきじゃない	げんきだった	げんきじゃなかった
しずかな (quiet)	しずか	しずかじゃない	しずかだった	しずかじゃなかった
ひまな (not busy)	ひま	ひまじゃない	ひまだった	ひまじゃなかった
あんぜんな (safe)	あんぜん	あんぜんじゃない	あんぜんだった	あんぜんじゃなかった
きけんな (dangerous)	きけん	きけんじゃない	きけんだった	きけんじゃなかった
かんたんな (easy)	かんたん	かんたんじゃない	かんたんだった	かんたんじゃなかった
たいせつな (important)	たいせつ	たいせつじゃない	たいせつだった	たいせつじゃなかった
まじめな (serious)	まじめ	まじめじゃない	まじめだった	まじめじゃなかった
ふくざつな (complicated)	ふくざつ	ふくざつじゃない	ふくざつだった	ふくざつじゃなかった
しんせつな (kind)	しんせつ	しんせつじゃない	しんせつだった	しんせつじゃなかった

Practice 2

① 今日は<u>あつい</u>です。

② 日本語は<u>むずかしくない</u>です。

③ この時計は<u>たかい</u>です。

④ テストは<u>むずかしかった</u>です。

⑤ このピザは<u>おいしくない</u>です。

⑥ ジョンの家は<u>おおきい</u>です。

⑦ この街は<u>あんぜんじゃない</u>です。

Practice 3

①おおきいいえです。

②せまいみちです

③ふるいいえです。

④あたらしいスマホです

⑤おもしろいえいがです。

Practice 4 – Write your own answer

Practice 5

① きのうわたしのへやはきれいでした。

② きょうてんきがよくなかったです。

③ えいがはおもしろくなかったです。

④ たいせつなテストがありました。

⑤ くつはやすかったです。

⑥ いもうとはせがひくかったです。

⑦ おねえさんはかみがながかったです。

⑧ きのうひまでした。

⑨ ちゅうしゃじょうはひろいです。

⑩ このにほんごのじしょはたかくなかったです。

Practice 6

スカイ

①めがおおきいです

②あしがながいです

③かみがみじかいです

ノア

①あしがみじかいです

②からだがおおきいです

③かみがみじかいです

Practice 7 – Write your own answer

Practice 8

①サンディはげんきでかわいいです。

②ディアナはしずかであたまがいいです。

③ジョンはおもしろくてせがたかいです。

④アレックスはやさしくてまじめです

⑤トシはあたまがよくてやさしいです。

SECTION 3-3: LISTENING EXERCISES

 Practice 1

ここが僕の家です。最近、新しい家に引っ越しました。とても大きな家です。庭は広くてきれいです。でも僕の部屋はあまり広くありません。でも大きいテレビがあります。

① A

② C

③ D

Practice 2

ディアナ：サンディさんの好きな食べ物は何ですか？

サンディ：私はカレーライスが大好きです。

ディアナ：すしは好きですか？

サンディ：すしも好きです。でもさしみはあまり好きじゃないです。

ディアナ：サンディさんはスポーツが好きですか？

サンディ：はい、ハイキングが大好きです。

ディアナ：バスケットボールが好きですか？

サンディ：はい、でもあまり上手じゃないです。

① はい、サンディはカレーライスがだいすきです。

② はい、サンディはバスケットボールがすきです。

Practice 3

トシ：これが私のペットで、名前はペコといいます。

ディアナ：耳が大きくてかわいい犬ですね。

トシ：はい、ビーグル犬です。体は小さいですが、頭がいいんです。ディアナさんの犬はどんな犬ですか？

ディアナ：はい、私は大きな犬をかっています。名前はサミーです。とても力が強くてやさしい犬です。

トシ：すごいですね。こんど見せてください。

① False

② True

③ True

Practice 4

日本の神津島に行きました。毎日いい天気でしたが、とても暑かったです。ビーチがとてもきれいでしずかでした。ホテルは新しくありませんでしたが、きれいでした。朝ごはんもおいしかったです。サーフィンは難しかったです。

① ビーチはとてもきれいでしずかでした。

② ホテルはあたらしくありませんでした。

③ サーフィンはむずかしかったです。

LESSON 4

SECTION 3-1: VOCABULARY

Practice 1

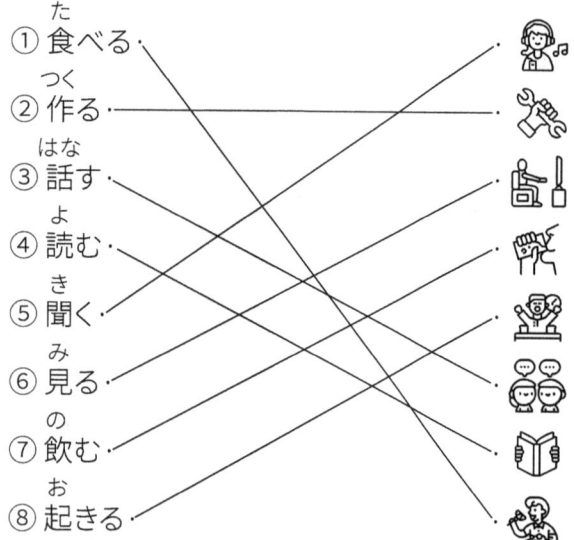

SECTION 3-2: READING AND WRITING

Practice 1

① *ru*-verbs

Dictionary form	Affirmative	Negative
Example: たべる　to eat	たべます	たべません
きる　to wear	きます	きません
ねる　to go to sleep	ねます	ねません
おきる　to wake	おきます	おきません
でかける　to go out	でかけます	でかけません
みる　to see	みます	みません
おしえる　to teach	おしえます	おしえません
あける　to open	あけます	あけません
しめる　to close	しめます	しめません

② *u*-verbs

Dictionary form	Affirmative	Negative
はなす　to speak	はなします	はなしません
きく　to listen	ききます	␣ききません
ひく　to play	ひきます	ひきません
およぐ　to swim	およぎます	およぎません
あそぶ　to hang out	あそびます	あそびません
のむ　to drink	のみます	のみません
よむ　to read	よみます	よみません
かう　to buy	かいます	かいません
いる　to need	いります	いりません

Japanese Grammar Made Easy | Answer Key

Practice 2

① A

② D

③ C

④ C

⑤ A

Practice 3

① ともだちとかいものにいきます。

② コーヒーショップでべんきょうします。

③ かぞくとはなします。

④ いえをそうじします。

⑤ おっととレストランにいきます。

⑥ いえでえいがをみます。

Practice 4

① にほんごのおんがくをききます。

② どようびにおよぎます。

③ よるごはんをつくります。

④ 6じにおきます。

⑤ サンディはいえでにほんごをはなします。

⑥ トシはスペインごをはなしません。

⑦ すいようびにアレックスはスタバにいきます。

⑧ ジョンは11じにねます。

⑨ ディアナはハンバーガーをたべません。

⑩ ノアはピアノをひきません。

Practice 5 – Write your own answer

Practice 6

① *ru*-verbs

Dictionary form	Past tense affirmative	Past tense negative
Example：たべる	たべました	たべませんでした
きる	きました	きませんでした
ねる	ねました	ねませんでした
おきる	おきました	おきませんでした
でかける	でかけました	でかけませんでした
みる	みました	みませんでした
おしえる	おしえました	おしえませんでした
あける	あけました	あけませんでした
しめる	しめました	しめませんでした

② *u*-verbs

Dictionary form	Past tense affirmative	Past tense negative
はなす	はなしました	はなしませんでした
きく	ききました	ききませんでした
ひく	ひきました	ひきませんでした
およぐ	およぎました	およぎませんでした
あそぶ	あそびました	あそびませんでした
のむ	のみました	のみませんでした
よむ	よみました	よみませんでした
かえる	かえりました	かえりませんでした
しゃべる	しゃべりました	しゃべりませんでした

Practice 7

① わたしは中学生です。
② わたしの父は６０才です。
③ 図書館にいきます。
④ 図書館で本を読みました。
⑤ 友だちの家で映画を見ました。
⑥ わたしはお茶を飲みます。
⑦ 自転車で郵便局に行きます。
⑧ 新幹線で大阪に行きます。
⑨ ７時に夜ご飯を食べます。
⑩ 友だちとサッカーをします。
⑪ 新しい服とくつを買いました。
⑫ タコスとサラダを食べました。
⑬ 友だちの家に泊まりました。
⑭ シカゴから来ました。
⑮ 集会は１０時から始まります。

Practice 8

Question 1: C
Question 2: B
Question 3: D
Question 4: A

SECTION 3-3: LISTENING EXERCISES

 Practice 1

① トシ
月曜日と火曜日は家で働きました。
水曜日は学校で日本語をおしえました。
木曜日は公園で散歩しました。金曜日は
妻とレストランに行きました。土曜日は買い
物に行きました。日曜日は家で休みました。

Question 1: がっこうでにほんごをおしえました。
Question 2: きんようびにレストランにいきました。

② サンディ
月曜日と水曜日は仕事をしました。火曜日
は部屋のそうじをしました。木曜日は買い
物に行きました。金曜日は映画を見ました。
土曜日は友だちの家に行きました。
日曜日はバスケットボールをしました。

Question 1: ともだちのいえにいきました。
Question 2: げつようびとすいようびです。

③ アレックス
今週は毎日学校で勉強しました。
金曜日は友だちと公園で遊びました。
土曜日は家族とキャンプに行きました。
日曜日は教会に行きました。

Question 1: ともだちとこうえんであそびました。
Question 2: にちようびです。

④ ディアナ
月曜日から金曜日まで毎日働きました。
金曜日の夜は友だちとレストランに行き
ました。土曜日はジムに行きました。
夜はパーティに行きました。日曜日は友
だちと家で映画を見ました。

Question 1: はたらきました。
Question 2: どようびです。

Practice 2

8時から仕事をします。10時にミーティングがあります。12時にディアナさんとランチを食べます。3時にコーヒーを飲みます。5時に家に帰ります。7時にレストランでカレーを食べます。9時に家でテレビを見ます。11時に寝ます。

Question 1: 8じからしごとをします。

Question 2: 5じにいえにかえります。

Question 3: レストランでカレーをたべます。

Question 4: 11じにねます。

LESSON 5

 SECTION 3-1: VOCABULARY

Practice 1

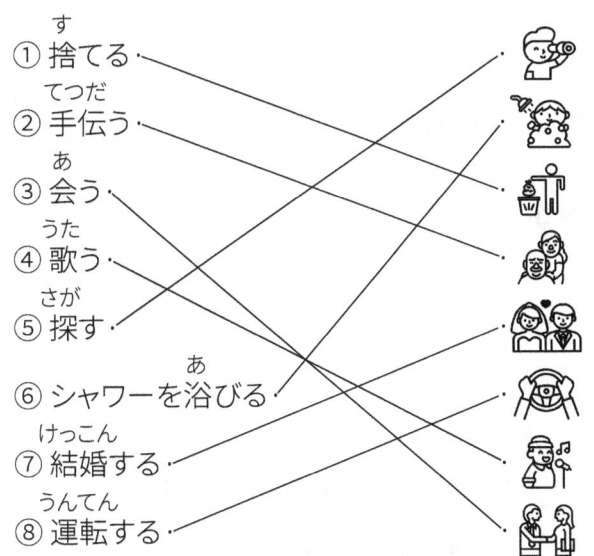

SECTION 3-2: READING AND WRITING

Practice 1

	te-form		te-form
きる　to wear	きて	はなす	はなして
おきる	おきて	きく	きいて
でかける	でかけて	てつだう	てつだって
みる	みて	あそぶ	あそんで
おしえる	おしえて	よむ	よんで
あける	あけて	とまる	とまって
しめる	しめて	うんてんする	うんてんして

Practice 2

① まどをしめてください。

② にほんごをおしえてください。

③ きいてください。

④ このきょうかしょをよんでください。

⑤ ゆっくりはなしてください。

⑥ まいにちピアノをれんしゅうしてください。

⑦ ごみをすててください。

⑧ あしたでんわしてください。

⑨ てつだってください。

⑩ このビデオをみてください。

Practice 3

① いすにすわってもいいですか？

② しゃしんをとってもいいですか？

③ ペンをつかってもいいですか？

④ えいごをはなしてもいいですか？

⑤ ギターをひいてもいいですか？

⑥ まどをしめてもいいですか？

⑦ トイレにいってもいいですか？

⑧ ドアをあけてもいいですか？

⑨ ごみをすててもいいですか？

⑩ ワインをのんでもいいですか？

Practice 4

① B　　② E　　③ C　　④ D　　⑤ A

Practice 5

① ノアはにほんりょうりをたべています。

② スカイはテニスをしています。

③ フアンはくるまをうんてんしています。

④ ディアナはよるごはんをつくっています。

⑤ サンディはにほんごをべんきょうしています。

⑥ トシはカラオケでうたっています。

⑦ ソアはギターをひいています。

⑧ ジョンはゲームをしています。

Practice 6

Question 1: カナダのバンクーバーにすんでいます。

Question 2: けいざいをべんきょうしています。

Question 3: まだけっこんしていません。

Question 4: アメリカのシカゴにすんでいます。

Question 5: びょういんではたらいています。

Question 6: どようびはジムでうんどうしています。にちようびはにほんごをべんきょうしています。

Practice 7

① 6じにおきて、あさごはんをたべます。

② あたらしいドレスをきて、パーティにいきます。

③ でんしゃにのって、とうきょうにいきます。

④ あさごはんをたべて、コーヒーをのみます。

⑤ ギターをひいて、うたをうたいます。

⑥ としょかんにいって、にほんごをべんきょうします。

⑦ テレビをみて、ねます。

⑧ あさごはんをつくって、そうじします。

Practice 8

① こうえんにいって、ほんをよみました。

② へやをそうじして、しゅくだいをしました。

③ ビールをのんで、うたをうたいました。

④ シャワーをあびて、レストランにいきました。

⑤ ともだちのいえにとまって、ビデオゲームをしました。

Practice 9

① 来年日本に行きます。もう飛行機のチケットを買いました。でもまだホテルは予約していません。

② A：もう薬をのみましたか？

　B：いいえ、まだのんでいません。でももう体調はよくなりました。

③ A：もうこのゲームを買いましたか？

　B：はい、もう買いました。でも、まだしていません。

Practice 10

① はい、もうしました。

② いいえ、まだおぼえていません。

③ いいえ、まだみつかっていません。

④ はい、もうかいました。

⑤ いいえ、まだあらっていません。

⑥ いいえ、まだはらっていません。

⑦ はい、もうでんわしました。

⑧ いいえ、まだよんでいません。

SECTION 3-3: LISTENING EXERCISES

 ## Practice 1

こんにちは、スカイです。わたしはアメリカ人です。学生の時は、コンピューターを勉強しました。2年前、日本にひっこして、今は大阪に住んでいます。英語の先生をしています。しゅみは読書とアニメです。日本のアニメが好きです。週末は日本語を勉強しています。もう漢字を500個おぼえました。

Question 1: にほんのおおさかにすんでいます。

Question 2: にほんのアニメがすきです。

Question 3: もう500こおぼえました。

 ## Practice 2

これは僕の家族の写真です。これがお父さんです。父は背が高いです。シドニーに住んでいます。銀行で働いています。母は生まれたばかりの妹を抱いています。母もシドニーに住んでいます。こちらは兄です。ニューヨークに住んでいます。銀行で働いています。日本人の女性と結婚しています。左手を上げているのは私の姉です。姉は大学生です。大学で法律を勉強しています。

① True

② False

③ False

④ False

LESSON 6

SECTION 3-1: VOCABULARY

Practice 1

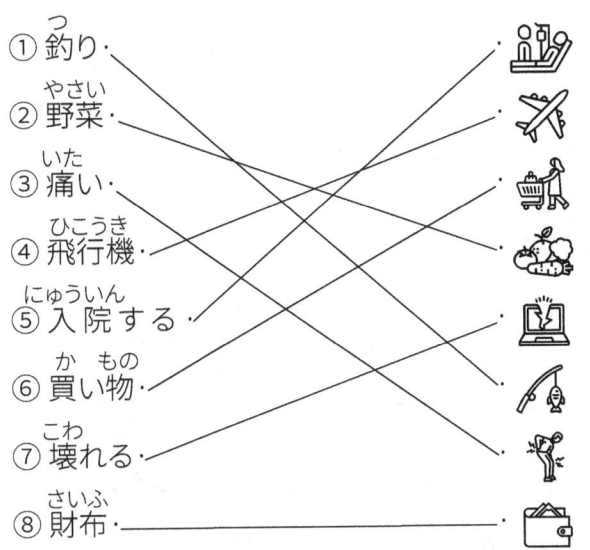

SECTION 3-2: READING AND WRITING

Practice 1

Dictionary form	Long form	Short form	Past tense short form
みる to see	みます	みる	みた
	みません	みない	みなかった
のむ to drink	のみます	のむ	のんだ
	のみません	のまない	のまなかった
ねる to sleep	ねます	ねる	ねた
	ねません	ねない	ねなかった
よむ to read	よみます	よむ	よんだ
	よみません	よまない	よまなかった
かく to write	かきます	かく	かいた
	かきません	かかない	かかなかった
はなす to speak	はなします	はなす	はなした
	はなしません	はなさない	はなさなかった
あらう to wash	あらいます	あらう	あらった
	あらいません	あらわない	あらわなかった
やすむ to rest	やすみます	やすむ	やすんだ
	やすみません	やすまない	やすまなかった
さがす to look for	さがします	さがす	さがした
	さがしません	さがさない	さがさなかった

Practice 2

① どんなおんがくをきく？

② よくバスにのる？

③ しゅうまつはなにをする？

④ もうあさごはんたべた？

⑤ もうしゅくだいおわった？

Practice 3

① あけない

② とらない

③ はしらない

④ いれない

⑤ すわない

Practice 4

① くるまをかうつもりです。

② レストランにいくつもりです。

③ スペインごをべんきょうするつもりです。

④ 9じにねるつもりです。

⑤ ジャケットをきるつもりです。

⑥ 日本でしごとをさがすつもりです。

⑦ あきにけっこんするつもりです。

⑧ にちようびははたらかないつもりです。

⑨ こんやはバーにいかないつもりです。

⑩ ケーキをたべないつもりです。

Practice 5

① ジムにいくつもりです。

② かいものにいくつもりです。

③ どようびはプールにいって、にちようびはえいがをみるつもりです。

④ はたらくつもりです。

Practice 6

① サンディはプールでおよぐとおもいます。

② シンジはハイキングにいくとおもいます。

③ アレックスはがくせいだとおもいます。

④ シカゴのふゆはさむいとおもいます。

⑤ エルサはにほんごをはなすとおもいます。

⑥ スカイはビールをのまないとおもいます。

⑦ トシはがくせいじゃないとおもいます。

⑧ フアンはあたらしいくるまをかわないとおもいます。

⑨ ディアナはにほんのアニメをみないとおもいます。

Practice 7

① カナダにいったことがあります。

② にほんりょうりをつくったことがあります。

③ そのおんがくをきいたことがあります。

④ ピアノをならったことがあります。

⑤ がいこくにすんだことがあります。

⑥ きょうとにいったことがありません。

⑦ りょうしんにてがみをかいたことがありません。

⑧ うみでおよいだことがありません。

⑨ そのほんをよんだことがありません。

⑩ そのえいがをみたことがありません。

Practice 8 – Write your own answer

Practice 9

① D　② A　③ D　④ B　⑤ C　⑥ A

Practice 10 - Write your own answer

Practice 11

① D　② B　③ C　④ B　⑤ B

Practice 12

① 音楽が好きだから、ピアノを習います。
② 飛行機は高いから、バスを使います。
③ 兄が結婚するから、プレゼントを買います。
④ 今日はあついから、プールで泳ぎます。
⑤ 友だちが家に来るから、部屋をそうじします。

Practice 13

① コーヒーをのんだから、ねむくないです。

② あしたテストがあるから、でかけません。

③ コンピューターがこわれたから、あたらしいコンピューターをかいます。

④ おかあさんはびょうきだから、くすりをかいました。

⑤ つかれたから、いえにかえります。

Practice 14 – Write your own answer

SECTION 3-3: LISTENING EXERCISES

 Practice 1

サンディ：先週、家族と一緒に京都に行ったよ。

ノア：へえ、どうだった？

サンディ：古いお寺や建物がたくさんあって、とてもきれいな町だったよ。京都に行ったことある？

ノア：ううん、行ったことないなあ。何を食べたの？

サンディ：天ぷらとラーメン、抹茶のスイーツを食べたよ。とてもおいしかったよ！

ノア：どうやって京都に行ったの？

サンディ：新幹線で行ったよ。でも新幹線は高いから、帰りはバスを使った。

ノア：いいね。新幹線はどうだった？

サンディ：とっても速かった！それに静かで快適だったよ。新幹線に乗ったことある？

ノア：うん、あるよ。2年前大阪に行ったんだ。

サンディ：いいね。大阪には行ったことないなあ。

Question 1: いいえ、いったことがありません。
Question 2: はい、しんかんせんにのったことがあります。
Question 3: いいえ、サンディはおおさかにいったことがありません。

 Practice 2

トシ：日本語の勉強はどうですか？

アレックス：楽しいです。でも漢字は難しいです。

トシ：そうですよね。日本語の本をたくさん読んだほうがいいですよ。

アレックス：わかりました。毎日ひとつ漢字をおぼえるつもりです。

トシ：いいですね。あと、日本人の友だちをつくったほうがいいですよ。覚えた日本語をどんどん使ってください。

アレックス：はい、がんばります。

① にほんごのほんをたくさんよんだほうがいいですよ。
② にほんじんのともだちをつくったほうがいいですよ。

LESSON 7

SECTION 3-1: VOCABULARY

Practice 1

① 薬局 (やっきょく)
② 温泉 (おんせん)
③ お金持ち (かねも)
④ 運転免許 (うんてんめんきょ)
⑤ 牛乳 (ぎゅうにゅう)
⑥ 日本酒 (にほんしゅ)
⑦ 警察 (けいさつ)
⑧ 翻訳 (ほんやく)

SECTION 3-2: READING AND WRITING

Practice 1

Short form	tai-form	
	affirmative	negative
いく	いきたい	いきたくない
やすむ	やすみたい	やすみたくない
なる	なりたい	なりたくない
あう	あいたい	あいたくない
はたらく	はたらきたい	はたらきたくない
りゅうがくする	りゅうがくしたい	りゅうがくしたくない
ならう	ならいたい	ならいたくない
のる	のりたい	のりたくない

Practice 2

① にほんごをべんきょうしたいです。

② かのじょとけっこんしたいです。

③ にほんにりゅうがくしたいです。

④ くるまをかいたいです。

Practice 3 – Write your own answer

Practice 4

① きゅうじつはいえでゆっくりしたいです。

② あついからプールでおよぎたいです。

③ しゃしんをとるのがすきだからあたらしいカメラがほしいです。

④ まいにちいそがしいからじかんがほしいです。

⑤ つかれたからいえでねたいです。

Practice 5

① 日本に行きたいから、日本語を勉強します。

② 運転免許をとったから、車を運転したいです。

③ 試験が終わったから、友だちと遊びたいです。

④ お金がないから、買い物に行きたくないです。

⑤ あついから、水を飲みたいです。

Practice 6

① しごとにいきたくないです。

② コーヒーをのみたいです。

③ やさいをたべたくないです。

④ おさけをのみたくないです。

⑤ シャワーをあびたくないです。

⑥ サッカーせんしゅになりたいです。

Practice 7

① ピアノをならいたかったです。

② ひこうきにのりたかったです。

③ ビデオゲームをしたかったです。

④ ペットがほしかったです。

⑤ カリフォルニアにいきたかったです。

⑥ そのえいがをみたくなかったです。

⑦ コーヒーをのみたくなかったです。

⑧ かれにあいたくなかったです。

⑨ りゅうがくしたくなかったです。

⑩ くるまをうんてんしたくなかったです。

⑪ パーティにいきたくなかったです。

Practice 8 – Write your own answer

Practice 9

① じてんしゃがほしいです。

② おかねがほしいです。

③ ビデオゲームがほしいです。

④ アイスクリームがほしいです。

Practice 10

① じしょはほしくないです。

② ぬいぐるみはほしくないです。

③ カメラはほしくないです。

④ プレゼントはほしくないです。

Practice 11 – Write your own answer

Practice 12

① サンディはきものをきたいといっています。

② ディアナはダンスパーティにいきたいといっています。

③ ジョンはおかねもちになりたいといっています。

④ アレックスはピアノをれんしゅしたくないといっています。

⑤ トシはにほんしゅをのみたいといっています。

Practice 13

① ディアナ

Question 1: B

Question 2: ともだちとディズニーランドであそびたいといっています。

② ジョン

Question 1: A

Question 2: ふるいおてらをみたいといっています。

Question 3: およぎたいそうです。

③ アレックス

Question 1: D

Question 2: にほんにりゅうがくしたいといっています。

④ サンディ

Question 1: C

Question 2: いぬとさんぽしたくないといっています。

Practice 14

① アレックスはともだちのいえにテレビゲームをしにいきます。

② トシはこうえんにさくらをみにいきます。

③ フアンはゆうびんきょくにてがみをだしにいきます。

④ スカイはコンビニにおにぎりをかいにいきます。

⑤ ノアはスタバにともだちにあいにいきます。

⑥ ジョンはやっきょくにくすりをかいにいきます。

SECTION 3-3: LISTENING EXERCISES

 Practice 1

スカイ：明日は休日だね。何をする？

ソア：仕事も休みだから、どこかに遊びに行きたいなあ。スカイは何をしたい？

スカイ：わたしは買い物に行きたいな。最近寒くなってきたから、新しいジャケットを買いたい。

ソア：いいね。私も新しい靴がほしい。

スカイ：じゃあ、いっしょに買い物に行こう。買い物のあとは何する？

ソア：カラオケはどう？歌いたい気分だなあ。

スカイ：いいね！

① False
② True
③ False

 Practice 2

明日から夏休み。したいことがたくさんあります。7月は家族でカリフォルニアに行きます。ビーチでたくさん泳ぎたいです。でもお母さんは泳ぎたくないと言っていました。お母さんはハイキングに行きたいそうです。お父さんは疲れているから、ビールを飲んでゆっくりしたいと言っていました。夏休みはあまり勉強したくないです。でも日本語は練習するつもりです。漢字を１００個おぼえたいと思います。

Question 1: べんきょうしたくないそうです。
Question 2: ビールをのんでゆっくりしたいそうです。
Question 3: かんじを１００こおぼえたいそうです。

MORE BOOKS BY LINGO MASTERY

We are not done teaching you Japanese until you're fluent!

Here are some other titles you might find useful in your journey of mastering Japanese

✓ Japanese Short Stories for Beginners

✓ Intermediate Japanese Short Stories

✓ 2000 Most Common Japanese Words in Context

✓ Conversational Japanese Dialogues

But we got many more!

Check out all of our titles at **www.lingomastery.com/japanese**

www.ingramcontent.com/pod-product-compliance
Lightning Source LLC
Chambersburg PA
CBHW081444070526
44586CB00019B/2221